# FATHER & SON

A Weekly Father-Son Devotional
to Build Character
and Faith in Teenage Boys

## OAK & ANCHOR PRESS

**Father & Son: A Weekly Father-Son Devotional to Build Character and Faith in Teenage Boys**

© 2026 Oak & Anchor Press



Published by Oak & Anchor Press

ISBNs:
eBook: 979-8-9953447-0-4
Paperback: 979-8-9953447-1-1
Hardcover: 979-8-9953447-2-8

First edition, 2026
Publication Date: May 31, 2026



This book is intended for educational and spiritual growth purposes. It is not a substitute for professional counseling, legal advice, or medical guidance.

Cover design and interior layout by independent contractors. All music and supplementary media associated with this work are produced under Oak & Anchor Press.

For more information, visit: oakanchorpress.com

To *The Spiritual Spotters*,

my brothers in study and in truth.


In learning to walk in Scripture,

I came to see what was always there-

that the Word of God is not foreign to man,

but the ground he was made to stand on.

# Theme Index

# Introduction

A father may stand outside his son's bedroom door and hesitate.

He intends to begin something good: a weekly time in Scripture, a conversation about faith and manhood. Yet questions gather quickly.

What if he resists?

What if it feels forced?

What if I do not know enough?

These concerns are not signs of failure; they are signs that the task matters.

Many fathers love their sons deeply and yet feel uncertain about where to begin in shaping them spiritually. Daily life is full, and conversations orbit around school, schedules, and responsibilities. Meanwhile, the deeper matters of belief, character, and calling remain largely unspoken. Such hesitation carries a cost.

Our age is not silent about manhood; it speaks constantly. It offers shifting definitions of strength, success, power, and identity. A young man is exposed to countless competing visions in a single hour. Few of them are patient, and fewer still are anchored in truth. Sons are not formed by noise; they are formed by presence, example, and steady instruction under God's Word. The question, then, is who will guide it.

## The Quiet Return

This book begins with something modest: a weekly return to Scripture. Choose a time. Protect it as you are able. Sit together. Open the Word of God. Read carefully. Speak plainly. Listen patiently. This rhythm, repeated week after week, accomplishes more than sporadic and dramatic efforts.

Order shapes the soul.

Regularity trains the heart.

A pattern, once established, becomes part of the household's moral architecture.

You are not called to impress your son with insight or theological mastery. You are called to place both of you under the authority of Scripture. Authority in the Christian life is not self-created; it is received from God and exercised under His Word. A father does not stand above the Word; he stands beneath it with his son.

There is a difference between raising a competent young man and raising a godly one. A father may model diligence, responsibility, and kindness. These are good gifts. Yet, without the steady presence of Scripture, the foundation remains incomplete. Cultural expectations, peer influence, and media narratives will supply their own definitions of manhood if a father does not provide a better one.

With Scripture as the foundation, something firmer emerges. A son learns that identity is received in Christ, not constructed by applause. He learns that strength is demonstrated through restraint and obedience, not impulse. He learns that authority is exercised under God, not apart from Him.

The fruit of this labor is often quiet and slow to mature. Yet, over time, a different kind of young man begins to develop. One who thinks carefully, acts deliberately, and understands that he stands under God's authority.

## A Word About Approach

This devotional rests on a simple conviction: Scripture is final and formative for Christian life and manhood. Young men tend to resist pressure and flourish under calm conviction. They close themselves off to manipulation and respond to steadiness. A father who combines clarity with composure teaches more than content; he teaches character. The structure of this book reflects that intention.

- Part One establishes rhythm and identity in Christ.

- Part Two strengthens discipline and stewardship.

- Part Three develops responsibility and integrity in the use of authority and resources.

- Part Four prepares for discernment, brotherhood, and legacy.

Each week provides guidance for both father and son. The progression is deliberate. We begin with posture and pattern, build toward strength and leadership, and conclude with endurance and long obedience. The four parts will be accompanied by a QR code leading to a song that reflects on each of these parts as a whole.

The first step is simple:

Set a time.

Open the Scriptures.

Read with care.

Return the following week.

There is no need to wait for the "right time"; you need only to begin. In time, what feels small will grow into something foundational. Order precedes strength; rhythm precedes resolve. A faithful presence under God's Word becomes a legacy that outlives you.

Begin today the steady work that will shape a legacy under God's Word.

# Part One:
## Establishing the Devotional Foundation

### Weeks 1–13

The foundation of a young man's character is not built through grand gestures or dramatic moments. It is formed in quiet, steady practices. Part One focuses on laying this foundation through a deliberate, simple rhythm anchored in Scripture.

Over these weeks, fathers will learn the value of steadfast presence. Sons will discover that faithfulness is shaped not by occasional excitement, but by repeated, patient encounters with God's Word.

The work is gradual and often unseen. Yet it establishes the groundwork for all that follows: a secure identity in Christ, moral formation, self-command, and the capacity for godly leadership. This is the beginning of a pattern that can endure for a lifetime.

♪ Scan to listen to "Stone by Stone"

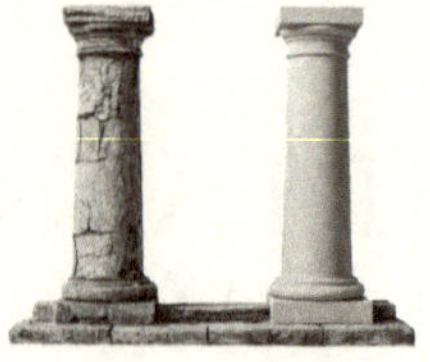



# CHAPTER 1

# INITIATING DEVOTIONS AND STEADFAST PRESENCE

Before a man can be courageous or discerning, he must first be consistent. Consistency is not the same as intensity, though we often confuse the two. Intensity rises quickly and speaks loudly. Consistency works quietly and endures. One depends upon feeling. The other on settled conviction.

The Christian life is sustained by habits that return us, again and again, to the Word of God. These habits are not empty routines. They are the ordinary means by which the Lord forms His people over time. Through repetition, the heart is trained. Through steady return, the mind is instructed. Through patient practice, character is shaped.

A weekly rhythm of shared devotion between father and son may become one such practice. This is not about putting on a show. It is about presence. It is about setting aside time, consistently and without excuse, to seek the Lord together. In doing so, a father reflects, in his limited and creaturely way, the faithfulness of God Himself, who keeps covenant, who does not withdraw when response is slow, and whose mercies endure.

The work begins simply. It continues steadily. With time, steadiness becomes formative.

## WEEK 1: THE RHYTHM OF FAITH

*Father's Reflection*

Forming a young man does not begin with a burst of resolve or a speech about noble intentions. It begins more quietly, with order. If a household is to be shaped and governed by the Word of God, that Word must be given a settled place within the home. Scripture and prayer cannot remain admirable ideas. They must be appointed realities.

The first responsibility of a father in this regard is a deliberate one. He must dedicate time to worship. Not in abstraction, but in practice. Choose a particular day and hour each week and set it apart for devotion. Let it be known, without fanfare, that this time belongs to the Lord. The greater difficulty lies in guarding that hour. Life does not suspend itself for sacred intentions. Duties multiply. Fatigue accumulates. Minor urgencies present themselves as reasonable excuses. Yet a father should treat this appointment as a settled commitment before God. Whether he realizes it or not, a man who governs his time declares what governs him. When Scripture is given a fixed place in the home, it is acknowledged as an authority rather than an accessory.

An appointment with God does not have to be a lengthy endeavor. The Lord is not honored by excess of words or elaborate display, but by sincerity and obedience. Twenty or 30 minutes, guarded from interruption and treated with seriousness, is sufficient to begin. What forms character is the regular return to Scripture. Steady exposure to the Word every week allows for the quiet work to start.

From ancient days, the people of God have worshiped at appointed times. Such patterns train the heart. They teach that meeting with the Lord is not accidental or casual. It is covenantal, shaped by obedience to what God has revealed.

In establishing a weekly rhythm of devotion, a father does more than fill a place in the schedule. He is showing the household that the Word of God orders the home.

Keep in mind that faith does not belong solely to moments of crisis. It inhabits ordinary weeks, when nothing dramatic occurs as well. An anchor serves little purpose if it is not set before the storm. In the same way, habits of worship must be established before difficulty tests them. Returning to Scripture each week teaches that God should be sought deliberately.

Actions, repeated with conviction, speak more clearly than declarations. The work may seem small at first. It may appear unremarkable. Yet what is ordinary, when repeated with faithfulness, becomes formative.

Begin plainly. Guard the hour. Return again next week. Let the rhythm stand.

*Scripture*

## 📖 Deuteronomy 6:4–9 (ESV)

Hear, O Israel: The LORD our God, the LORD is one. You shall love the LORD your God with all your heart and with all your soul and with all your might. And these words that I command you today shall be on your heart. You shall teach them diligently to your children, and shall talk of them when you sit in your house, and when you walk by the way, and when you lie down, and when you rise. You shall bind them as a sign on your hand, and they shall be as frontlets between your eyes. You shall write them on the doorposts of your house and on your gates.

*Son's Reflection*

A life of faith is not formed all at once. It grows through a steady return to God and His Word. Scripture teaches that we are to love the Lord with all our heart, soul, and strength, and that His commands should shape the rhythms of daily life. This kind of devotion is not created by a single moment of excitement. It develops through repeated choices to seek God again and again.

Setting aside time each week to read Scripture and pray may seem simple. Some weeks may feel ordinary. You may not notice change immediately. But the habits you practice consistently begin to shape your heart and mind over time. Listening to God's Word and thinking carefully about it teaches patience, humility, and trust.

Faithfulness is often quiet. The Lord does not measure devotion by how impressive it appears to others. He sees the heart. Choosing to meet with Him regularly shows that His Word matters and that His authority is welcomed in your life.

Strong faith is built through steady habits. Each time you return to God's Word, you are strengthening a foundation that will guide you in both calm seasons and difficult ones.

*Conversation Points*

- Why is a regular habit important in shaping character?
- What does it communicate when God's Word is given a fixed place in the home?
- What day and time will we set apart each week?
- How can we guard this time faithfully?

## Week 2: Consistency Over Perfection

*Father's Reflection*

Once a rhythm has been established, it will be tested. Some weeks will feel ordinary. Others will be strained by shifting schedules and competing demands. None of this is unusual. Ordinary does not mean unfruitful. Much of Christian growth unfolds quietly. There are seasons when no visible progress appears, yet obedience remains obedience, even when it feels unimpressive.

The soil of character is often tilled beneath the surface. Roots deepen long before fruit appears. A father must learn to value what is steady over what is visible, trusting that unseen formation is not wasted effort but necessary preparation. Perfection is not the measure of faithfulness. Scripture calls for steadfastness, not flawlessness. There will be weeks missed. There will be interruptions. There may be fatigue, distraction, or simple neglect. In those moments, indifference tempts withdrawal, and discouragement tempts surrender. Both erode discipline and quietly weaken resolve.

The proper response is simpler, but more demanding.

Return.

No excuses or dramatizing failure. A father must model this steadiness, teaching by example that constancy does not collapse under interruption.

The Lord's mercies are not diminished by human inconsistency. He remains faithful to His covenant promises, unchanging in His character and sure in His Word. In light of that faithfulness, devotion must not depend on mood, convenience, or emotional intensity. Character is not formed by isolated moments of zeal, but by repeated submission to what is right. Worship is an act of trust. It confesses that God works over time, often beyond what can be measured within a single week or season. A father who returns consistently, even after interruption, demonstrates that obedience is not fragile. It is sustained by conviction.

Guard against pride when the pattern holds. Guard against defeat when it falters. Resume the work.

Let faithfulness define the standard.

*Scripture*

## 📖 Galatians 6:7–10 (ESV)

Do not be deceived: God is not mocked, for whatever one sows, that will he also reap. For the one who sows to his own flesh will from the flesh reap corruption, but the one who sows to the Spirit will from the Spirit reap eternal life. And let us not grow weary of doing good, for in due season we will reap, if we do not give up. So then, as we have opportunity, let us do good to everyone, and especially to those who are of the household of faith.

*Son's Reflection*

Scripture teaches that a man reaps what he sows. Seeds planted faithfully will produce a harvest in their proper time. Growth does not appear immediately. First, the seed is planted. Then roots develop where no one can see them. Only later does the fruit become visible.

The same is true for spiritual habits. Reading Scripture, praying, and returning to God each week may feel repetitive. Some weeks will go well. Other weeks may feel rushed or distracted. Sometimes a routine will be interrupted. These moments do not mean failure. What matters most is the decision to begin again.

Consistency matters more than perfection. The Lord works through steady obedience, even when progress feels slow. Returning to what is right after stopping for a time shows perseverance and humility. Over time, these repeated choices shape your character.

Growth comes through persistence. When you continue in what is good, even after interruptions, you are building the kind of faith that endures.

*Conversation Points*

- Why is it easy to abandon habits when they are interrupted?

- What does perseverance teach about character?

- Why is returning more important than being perfect?

# Week 3: A Sacred Space

*Father's Reflection*

The Lord is present in all places at all times. He is not confined by walls or limited by geography. Yet people are not so constant. We are creatures formed by pattern, habit, and environment. What surrounds us often shapes our attention before a word is spoken. Disorder invites distraction. Noise competes for thought. Familiar routines easily overtake sacred intention. For this reason, the place of devotion matters.

Choose a place that is quiet, orderly, and free from interruption. Silence what can be silenced. Remove what does not belong to the purpose of the hour. Allow the setting itself to communicate that this time is distinct. It is not a place for casual conversation or passing routine, but one set apart for earnest reflection and the reading of Scripture.

The space does not need to be impressive. It need not be large or adorned with decoration. The Lord looks not at outward display but at the posture of the heart. A simple chair near a window, a cleared table in the corner of a room, or a small desk kept in order is sufficient. The aim is not atmosphere for its own sake, but attentiveness. What matters is that both the time and the place are guarded from distraction and excuse.

Return to this place week after week with the same seriousness of intent. The body learns through repetition, and the mind often follows where the body has been trained to go. Over time, the setting itself becomes associated with reflection, restraint, and the hearing of God's Word. Familiarity, when ordered rightly, strengthens focus rather than weakening it.

Setting aside a sacred space for devotion is not an act of superstition. It does not grant holiness to wood or walls. It is discipline. Order in the environment assists order in the soul. A father who prepares and maintains such a place shows his son that approaching God's Word is not casual. It is deliberate, thoughtful, and worthy of preparation.

Guard the space. Keep it simple. Return to it faithfully. Let its quiet order reinforce what you seek to cultivate within.

*Scripture*

## 📖 Ecclesiastes 5:1–2 (ESV)

Guard your steps when you go to the house of God. To draw near to listen is better than to offer the sacrifice of fools, for they do not know that they are doing evil. Be not rash with your mouth, nor let your heart be hasty to utter a word before God, for God is in heaven and you are on earth. Therefore let your words be few.

*Son's Reflection*

Approaching God and His Word is a serious and meaningful act. Scripture reminds us to draw near to listen carefully rather than rushing in with careless words. When something is important, we prepare ourselves to give it our full attention.

Having a quiet place for devotion can help you focus and remove distractions. The place itself is not what makes the time meaningful, but it helps create an environment where your mind and heart are ready to listen. When noise, clutter, and interruptions are reduced, it becomes easier to think about what Scripture teaches.

Returning to the same place week after week builds a helpful habit. Over time, that place becomes associated with reflection, learning, and prayer. What begins as a simple practice becomes a reminder that seeking God deserves careful attention.

Reverence grows through preparation. When you approach God calmly and thoughtfully, you are learning to respect His Word and listen with humility.

*Conversation Points*

- What does it mean to "draw near to listen" rather than to speak quickly?

- How does preparation influence the way we approach serious matters?

- What qualities should mark the place where we meet for devotion?

## WEEK 4: INVITING, NOT FORCING

*Father's Reflection*

Visible eagerness is not always a reliable sign of spiritual growth. Much that is genuine in a young man is restrained in outward expression. A father may hope to see enthusiasm when the Scriptures are opened, some spark of recognition or delight. Yet it is a mistake to measure maturity by animation. Depth often moves quietly. Roots extend beneath the soil long before any sign appears above it.

Within a Christian home, authority is real, but it is not harsh. It does not coerce what only God can awaken. Authority in the household stands beneath a higher authority. The father does not preside over Scripture as its master, nor does he wield it as an instrument of pressure. He stands under it. He answers to it. He is judged by the same Word he reads. His son sees not a ruler over the text, but a man governed by it.

Devotion is a reverent matter. Order is necessary. The appointed hour should be kept. The passage should be read. Attention should be given. But the tone must remain composed. A demanding spirit can provoke outward compliance while hardening the inward man. A steady and measured presence does more to invite engagement than repeated insistence. Ask thoughtful questions and allow time for response. Silence will sometimes settle into the room. The urge to rush in and fill it may arise, especially if a father fears indifference. Yet silence does not always signal resistance. It may be the space in which thought begins. Patience guards against mistaking quiet for coldness.

Faith cannot be forced into existence. It is not produced by pressure, nor secured by raised voices or sharpened expectations. It grows according to the mysterious working of God. A father's task is more restrained and more demanding. He is to cultivate steadiness. He prepares the ground through order, humility, and consistency. He tends the practice without presuming to command the result. When a father remains present, measured, and faithful week after week, trust is strengthened. The home becomes a place where Scripture is neither weapon nor ornament, but authority. Such constancy allows conviction to arise without compulsion.

Guard against irritation. Guard against performance. Maintain order. Practice patience as a virtue. Leave room for the quiet work of God, who alone gives growth.

*Scripture*

## 📖 Colossians 3:18–21 (ESV)

Wives, submit yourselves to your husbands, as is fitting in the Lord. Husbands, love your wives, and do not be harsh with them. Children, obey your parents in everything, for this pleases the Lord. Fathers, do not provoke your children, lest they become discouraged.

*Son's Reflection*

Learning about God and His Word takes time. Growth does not always happen quickly, and understanding often develops slowly. Scripture teaches us that authority in the home should be exercised with patience and care. What is truly strong does not need to be loud. It is steady and restrained.

Honest conversation about faith is easier when there is trust. When questions are welcomed and mistakes are not mocked, it becomes easier to speak openly and think carefully. Patience allows understanding to develop step by step.

Sometimes silence is part of the learning process. Taking time to think before answering can help you reflect more deeply on what Scripture teaches. A calm and respectful environment makes it easier to consider serious questions about faith, character, and obedience.

*Conversation Points*

- Why might pressure hinder honest discussion?
- How can we grow in listening as well as speaking?
- What would make this time meaningful and consistent?

## What We're Building in These First Four Weeks

These opening weeks establish something deeper than a habit. They lay foundations of trust. A son who sees his father return consistently to Scripture begins to associate faith with steadiness rather than impulse. He learns that God's Word is not ornamental. It is not brought forward for appearance or emphasis. It governs. It sustains. It is the appointed nourishment of the Christian life.

Within this rhythm, a father offers a visible pattern of constancy. He does not mirror God's faithfulness in fullness, yet he reflects something of its steadiness. He returns even when the response is slow. He continues even when visible progress is slight. In doing so, he shows that devotion is not dependent on immediate reward.

Before strength can be tested, order must be formed. Before leadership is exercised, submission must be learned. Before discernment matures, attention must be trained. These foundations are not dramatic, but they are decisive.

Begin simply. Continue faithfully.

Steadfast presence is the first lesson in manhood.

# CHAPTER 2

# Engaging God's Word: Hearing, Understanding, and Obeying

A man may read Scripture every day and remain unchanged if he does not stand under it in humility. Words recited insincerely cannot be truly received. Familiarity may dull the edge of conviction. The danger arises not only from neglect but from casual devotion. Scripture is not a tool to be managed. It is the revealed Word of the living God. It is authoritative and binding. To approach it reverently is to recognize that we are the ones addressed by it. Scripture speaks, and we answer.

To hear rightly requires more than repetition. It requires understanding and obedience. A man grows not by handling the Word, but by standing under it as one accountable to its authority.

## WEEK 5: STANDING UNDER THE AUTHORITY OF SCRIPTURE

*Father's Reflection*

Scripture is not advice, nor is it commentary offered for consideration. It is the Word of God. As such, it carries final authority over a man's belief and conduct. It does not compete with other voices, and it does not wait for approval. It speaks with the authority of the One who gives it. A father must first settle this conviction within himself. If he treats the Bible as negotiable, his son will learn to negotiate with it. If he handles it as a resource to reinforce his own conclusions, he teaches defiance. If he quotes it selectively to strengthen his preferences, he trains his son to do the same. But if he stands beneath it, corrected and instructed by it, he models humility before God.

The authority of Scripture is final and formative. It is not revised by cultural preference or softened by personal opinion. It is not adjusted to preserve comfort. It shapes conscience, identity, and action. It trains judgment. It steadies conviction. It exposes error. It builds wisdom. Scripture is binding because it speaks with God's authority, not our own.

This authority will, at times, confront personal assumptions. It will challenge long-held habits. It will expose pride, impatience, selfish ambition, and misplaced priorities. A father must be willing to acknowledge such correction openly and admit that Scripture has rebuked him is not weakness. It is strength rightly ordered. It shows that he is governed before he governs. A son who sees his father corrected by Scripture learns that manhood does not begin with independence. It begins with obedience. He learns that authority in the home is not self-generated, but derived and accountable. He learns that strength is not the refusal to bend, but the willingness to bow before God.

We do not master Scripture. Scripture masters us. That order must remain clear within the home, for from it flows humility, stability, and trust.

*Scripture*

### 📖 Psalm 119:129–136 (ESV)

Your testimonies are wonderful; therefore my soul keeps them. The unfolding of your words gives light; it imparts understanding to the simple. I open my mouth and pant, because I long for your commandments. Turn to me and be gracious to me, as is your way with those who love your name. Keep steady my steps according to your promise, and let no iniquity get dominion over me. Redeem me from man's oppression, that I may keep your precepts. Make your face shine upon your servant, and teach me your statutes. My eyes shed streams of tears, because people do not keep your law.

## Son's Reflection

The Bible is not just another book of advice. It is God's Word, and because it comes from Him, it carries authority over our lives. When we read Scripture, we are not deciding whether it is right or wrong. Instead, Scripture examines us. It reveals what is true about our thoughts, motives, and actions.

Sometimes God's Word confirms what we already believe. Other times, it corrects us. It may challenge our attitudes, expose selfishness, or call us to change a habit. These moments are important because they show whether we are willing to trust God's wisdom more than our own. Standing under Scripture means receiving both encouragement and correction with humility. It means believing that God's instructions are good, even when they are difficult to follow. A man who learns to accept correction from God's Word grows in maturity and wisdom.

God's Word is meant to guide your life, not simply inform your mind. True growth happens when you listen carefully and respond with obedience.

## Conversation Points

- What does it mean to stand under Scripture rather than over it?

- How can we recognize when we are using Scripture to support ourselves rather than submitting to it?

- Why does obedience demonstrate that we truly believe what we read?

## Week 6: Reading in Context and With Care

*Father's Reflection*

A man reveals the state of his soul by how he handles the Word of God. To approach the Bible with a careless spirit is an act of self-assertion rather than submission. Scripture is not a collection of isolated verses designed to validate our preferences; it is a divine revelation given with specific purpose, structure, and intent. To read responsibly is to recognize that God spoke through distinct authors, in particular times, to address real situations. When a man ignores these boundaries, he does not honor the Bible's authority; he subverts it.

The discipline of "context" is an exercise in humility. To read with care, a father must look at what comes before and after a passage. He must consider the flow of thought and the audience addressed. Words must be understood as they were given, tethered to their original meaning.

Before a man draws a conclusion or offers an application to his son, he must first perform the quiet work of observation. He should ask: *What words are repeated? What commands are actually given? What promises are truly made?* This careful observation reins in the imagination and keeps interpretation anchored to the written Word. It prevents the use of scattered phrases to create falsehoods. When the Word is handled with gravity, it becomes a mirror for the heart.

Patience in reading breeds a measured spirit. A father who trains himself to handle the Truth with care will find that he grows more deliberate in his speech, his discipline, and his decision-making. The man who is hasty with the Word is often hasty with his temper; the man who is precise with Scripture is often precise with his integrity.

The supreme authority of the Bible does not excuse a casual approach; on the contrary, that authority demands the highest reverence. To read slowly and thoughtfully is not an act of academic pride. It is a fundamental act of respect for the Father who spoke, ensuring that when we lead our sons, we are pointing them toward God's truth rather than our own echoes.

*Scripture*

### 📖 2 Timothy 2:14–19 (ESV)

Remind them of these things, and charge them before God not to quarrel about words, which does no good, but only ruins the hearers. Do your best to present yourself to God as one approved, a worker who has no need to be ashamed, rightly handling the word of truth. But avoid irreverent babble, for it will lead people into more and more ungodliness, and their talk will spread like gangrene. Among them are Hymenaeus and Philetus, who have swerved from the truth, saying that the resurrection has already happened. They are upsetting the faith of some. But God's firm foundation stands, bearing this seal: "The Lord knows those who are his," and, "Let everyone who names the name of the Lord depart from iniquity."

*Son's Reflection*

It can be tempting to rush through Scripture and look for a quick idea or encouraging phrase. But the Bible was not written to be skimmed quickly. It was written to be understood carefully. Reading with attention shows respect for what God has said. One important way to do this is by reading passages in their context. That means paying attention to the verses before and after the part you are studying. It also means asking what the author was explaining and why the passage was written. These steps help us understand God's intended meaning instead of forcing our own ideas into the text.

Learning to read carefully takes patience. Sometimes you must slow down and think about what the passage actually says before deciding what it means. This discipline trains your mind to be thoughtful and careful. A man who learns to handle Scripture with patience and respect becomes more measured in his words and decisions. When you take the time to read thoughtfully, you allow God's truth to guide your thinking.

*Conversation Points*

- Why does context matter when reading Scripture?
- What is the difference between observing a passage and applying it?
- How can careful reading protect us from misjudgment?

## WEEK 7: FROM HEARING TO OBEDIENCE

*Father's Reflection*

Often, men fall prey to the modern delusion that possessing information equates to possessing character. Insight divorced from action is not only useless; it is dangerous. Scripture was never intended to be a repository of abstract ideas for the curious mind to examine. It is a divine instrument of transformation, meant to govern the "moral imagination" and order the inner life of a man. A particular kind of vanity grows in the heart of a man who knows much of the Word, but does little with it. He may appear mature, draping himself in the language of the faith, but if his will remains unbent and his habits unchanged, he is living a falsehood. Such a man treats the commands of God as suggestions to be debated rather than laws to be obeyed.

Genuine obedience rarely relies on the theater of drama or the surge of a temporary feeling to carry its meaning. Scripture ordinarily changes a man through the steady, unspectacular submission of the will. While deep conviction may at times stir the emotions, the true measure of a man's faith is not found in his "paroxysms of feeling," but in his consistent presence under God's authority.

A man who hears and obeys is like a builder who anchors his house upon the bedrock of reality. Each act of obedience, however small, strengthens the architecture of his integrity. The man who hears the Truth and neglects it invites a slow hardening of the heart. To ignore the Word is to choose a state of spiritual atrophy.

Obedience is the mark of the mature man. Freedom is found in faithful adherence to the Word that gives life.

*Scripture*

### 📖 James 1:22–27 (ESV)

But be doers of the word, and not hearers only, deceiving yourselves. For if anyone is a hearer of the word and not a doer, he is like a man who looks intently at his natural face in a mirror. For he looks at himself and goes away and at once forgets what he was like. But the one who looks into the perfect law, the law of liberty, and perseveres, being no hearer who forgets but a doer who acts, he will be blessed in his doing. If anyone thinks he is religious and does not bridle his tongue but deceives his heart, this person's religion is worthless. Religion that is pure and undefiled before God the Father is this: to visit orphans and widows in their affliction, and to keep oneself unstained from the world.

## Son's Reflection

It is a mistake to believe that knowing the right answer is the same thing as being the right kind of man. In a classroom, we are often rewarded for having the correct information. But a life of faith works differently. Scripture teaches that we must be doers of the Word, not hearers only. That means the truth we learn must shape the way we live.

It is possible to understand a passage clearly and still ignore what it requires. A person might memorize verses or explain their meaning, yet refuse to obey them. When knowledge stays in the mind but never reaches the heart or actions, it does not produce real growth.

Obedience usually begins with small decisions. Choosing honesty when it would be easier to hide the truth. The finished chore that no one thanked you for. Speaking with self-control during a disagreement. These quiet choices build character. Each act of obedience strengthens your resolve. What feels difficult at first becomes easier through practice. In due time, repeated obedience forms habits that shape the kind of man you become.

Faith grows stronger when truth moves from understanding to action. The man who obeys God's Word builds a life that is steady and trustworthy.

## Conversation Points

- Why is knowledge without obedience dangerous?

- What small acts of obedience shape character over time?

- How does repeated obedience strengthen conviction?

# WEEK 8: CONVERSATION THAT FORMS MEN

*Father's Reflection*

Conversation is more than a means of relaying information; it is the laboratory of the soul. One must recognize that Scripture is a living authority, and as such, it is meant to be discussed, considered, and applied through the medium of serious dialogue. This is particularly true in the relationship between a father and his son. The home should be the primary space where the "moral imagination" is tutored through the art of the spoken word. However, the efficacy of this formation depends entirely upon the father's ability to maintain a steady, patient, and non-performative presence.

Consider the difference in the architecture of a home where a father asks a thoughtful question and waits in the silence for a response, versus one where the father demands an immediate, "correct" answer. The former invites reflection and honors the son's developing mind; the latter encourages a performance. When a man is impatient for a response, he signals to his son that the goal of their time together is efficiency or outward compliance. When a man allows for silence, he models a masculine restraint that is tempered by discipline. He demonstrates that he values the process of discernment.

To listen without interruption is an act of high discipline. It requires a man to check his own ego and his desire to constantly "fix" or "instruct." To receive a difficult or skeptical question from a son without showing irritation requires a deep-seated humility. Disagreement, when handled with a calm and measured spirit, does not undermine a father's authority; rather, it models strength under control. It shows the son that truth is robust enough to withstand questioning and that a man of character does not need to resort to anger to defend his convictions.

Encourage an honest wrestling with the difficult passages of the Word. Questions are not threats to the faith when they are approached with reverence; they are often the very means by which understanding deepens and becomes personal. The objective in these weekly conversations is never to "win" an argument or to extract a forced confession of belief. The goal is the formation of sound judgment. Steady, honest, and sober conversation conducted under the final authority of Scripture is the slow, certain way to shape a son's discernment. By practicing this measured dialogue, we move past the superficial and begin the long-term work of building a man who can think, speak, and act with the gravity that his calling requires.

*Scripture*

## 📖 Proverbs 18:13 (ESV)

Whoever isolates himself seeks his own desire; he breaks out against all sound judgment. A fool takes no pleasure in understanding, but only in expressing his opinion. When wickedness comes, contempt comes also, and with dishonor comes disgrace. The words of a man's mouth are deep waters; the fountain of wisdom is a bubbling brook. It is not good to be partial to the wicked or to deprive the righteous of justice. A fool's lips walk into a fight, and his mouth invites a beating. A fool's mouth is his ruin, and his lips are a snare to his soul. The words of a whisperer are like delicious morsels; they go down into the inner parts of the body. Whoever is slack in his work is a brother to him who destroys. The name of the Lord is a strong tower; the righteous man runs into it and is safe. A rich man's wealth is his strong city, and like a high wall in his imagination. Before destruction a man's heart is haughty, but humility comes before honor. If one gives an answer before he hears, it is his folly and shame.

*Son's Reflection*

Learning to speak and listen well is an important part of growing into manhood. Conversation is not only about sharing opinions. It is a way to think carefully about truth and to understand others. Scripture teaches that a wise person listens before answering and values understanding more than winning an argument.

Talking about Scripture with your father provides a place to practice this kind of thoughtful conversation. You can ask questions, consider difficult ideas, and learn how to explain what you believe. These discussions are not about giving the fastest or most impressive answer. They are about learning to think carefully and speak with respect. Listening is an important part of this process. When you slow down and truly hear what someone else is saying, you gain understanding. You also show humility, which is necessary for wisdom.

Honest conversations build discernment. You learn to tell the difference between shallow opinions and truth that is grounded in Scripture. This ability will guide your decisions and relationships as you grow older.

*Conversation Points*

- How does listening strengthen understanding?

- Why is patience important in serious conversation?

- What makes discussion under Scripture different from ordinary debate?

## What We're Building in These Weeks

Scripture stands above us, not beside us. By refusing to rush or to strip verses of their context, a man demonstrates that he values God's intended meaning over his own immediate convenience or emotional preference. The transition from hearing to doing is the true threshold of manhood. Obedience serves as the only honest measure of maturity. A man may possess a vast library of theological knowledge, but if his will remains unbent by the commands of Christ, he remains a spiritual infant.

The man who learns to stand under God's Word is the only man truly prepared to exercise leadership over others. In the biblical order, authority in the world must be tempered and shaped by a prior obedience before God. To attempt to lead others without first being led by the Spirit is an act of pride.

# BIBLICAL MANHOOD

Man lives according to what he believes himself to be. If his understanding of manhood is shaped by competition, appearance, or cultural noise, his character may bend toward instability. If it is shaped and guided by Scripture, he will grow in steadiness. Strength is not the starting line of manhood. Identity is.

A father who affirms his son's identity in Christ corrects distorted models of masculinity. Sons learn that the measure of true manhood lies in Christlike character, not displays of dominance. Identity comes before action, but purpose flows from belonging.

# WEEK 9: MADE IN GOD'S IMAGE

## Father's Reflection

Man is made in the image of God. This is the foundational truth of Scripture. Worth is given by God, not earned by achievement or effort. To build manhood on anything other than creation itself is to construct on shifting sand. A young man who understands he is made by God learns gratitude before ambition. He comes to see that identity is not something to be proven, but something to be received, stewarded, and reflected in daily life. This knowledge anchors decisions, shapes confidence, and guides conduct. Identity in God's image comes first; purpose, achievement, and influence flow from it. Without this foundation, effort may seek applause rather than to honor God.

The world, however, measures value differently. Skill, influence, appearance, and accomplishment are often seen as markers of manhood. Social recognition and measurable success can easily mislead, offering temporary satisfaction while failing to establish a firm sense of self. None of these external indicators confer the dignity inherent in God's design. A father's voice, echoing the truth of Scripture, is essential in countering these messages. Reminding a son that he is deliberately created by God protects him from both pride and despair. Pride forgets the Giver, claiming honor that is not rightfully his; despair forgets the gift, doubting worth that has already been bestowed.

When a father consistently affirms the truth—that man is created in the image of God—he nurtures a son who understands that manhood is not measured by achievement. Creation itself becomes a reminder that God's design is deliberate, sufficient, and sustaining. To know one's worth in God's eyes is a lesson in living faithfully, leading responsibly, and growing steadily in character. True manhood is rooted in this recognition.

## Scripture

### 📖 Genesis 1:27–31 (ESV)

So God created man in his own image, in the image of God he created him; male and female he created them. And God blessed them. And God said to them, "Be fruitful and multiply and fill the earth and subdue it and have dominion over the fish of the sea and over the birds of the heavens and over every living thing that moves on the earth." And God saw everything that he had made, and behold, it was very good. And there was evening and there was morning, the sixth day.

## Son's Reflection

Being made in God's image means your life has meaning from the very beginning. You were created intentionally, and your worth does not depend on how successful, talented, or popular you become. The world often tells people to measure themselves by comparison, but Scripture teaches something far more stable. Your value comes from God Himself.

Understanding this truth removes a heavy burden. You do not have to spend your life trying to prove that you matter. Instead, you can focus on growing into the person God designed you to be. When your identity is grounded in God's design, success becomes something to steward rather than something that defines you. This truth also shapes how you treat other people. Every person you meet carries the dignity of being made in God's image. That means respect, patience, and kindness are not optional qualities. They are responses to the value God has already placed on every human life.

When a young man understands that he is made in God's image, he learns to live with gratitude, humility, and confidence. He no longer needs to chase approval because he already knows where his true value comes from.

## Conversation Points

- What does it mean to be made in God's image?

- How does this truth protect us from pride?

- How does it protect us from discouragement?

## WEEK 10: CALLED TO PURPOSE

*Father's Reflection*

God creates intentionally, and He calls His people with intention as well. Purpose is not a self-invented ambition or a personal status symbol. It is faithful stewardship of what God entrusts. Gifts, abilities, and opportunities are not mere advantages or blessings along the way; they are responsibilities entrusted for service. A father must guide his son to see work as dignified, whether visible or quiet, celebrated or unseen. Every task done faithfully honors God. Vocation is broader than career. It may include responsibilities in the home, the community, and the church. A young man discovers his calling not through pressure or comparison, but through obedience in ordinary responsibilities. Faithfulness in small, present tasks prepares him for larger opportunities that will arise.

Purpose is received, not invented. God's call often precedes clarity. A young man may not yet know the full scope of his gifts or opportunities, but faithfulness in what is entrusted now cultivates the discernment to handle what will come. Status fades; service remains. Ambition without obedience leads to frustration, but obedience to God's call builds confidence, wisdom, and integrity.

A father should model this stewardship in his own life. Show attentiveness to responsibilities. Demonstrate diligence in unseen work. Express gratitude for tasks entrusted by God. Let his son witness the difference between working for recognition and working for God's glory. Purpose is inseparable from obedience, and obedience nurtures discernment. In guiding a son toward God's calling, emphasize service over acclaim, patience over impulse, and faithfulness over self-promotion. Teach that purpose flows from belonging to God and participating in His work. The foundation of manhood is not achievement; it is responsibility received and faithfully carried.

*Scripture*

### 📖 1 Corinthians 12:4–11 (ESV)

> Now there are varieties of gifts, but the same Spirit; and there are varieties of service, but the same Lord; and there are varieties of activities, but it is the same God who empowers

them all in everyone. To each is given the manifestation of the Spirit for the common good. For to one is given through the Spirit the utterance of wisdom, and to another the utterance of knowledge according to the same Spirit, to another faith by the same Spirit, to another gifts of healing by the one Spirit, to another the working of miracles, to another prophecy, to another the ability to distinguish between spirits, to another various kinds of tongues, to another the interpretation of tongues. All these are empowered by one and the same Spirit, who apportions to each one individually as he wills.

## Son's Reflection

Purpose is not about chasing recognition or trying to impress others. It is about faithfully using the gifts, abilities, and opportunities that God places in your hands. Sometimes people feel pressure to discover their calling immediately. In reality, purpose usually becomes clear over time. It grows through obedience in small responsibilities. Doing your work carefully, helping others, and learning to serve faithfully prepare you for the opportunities that come later.

The gifts God gives are not meant only for personal success. They are meant to benefit others. When you begin to see your abilities as tools for service, your attitude toward work begins to change. Effort becomes meaningful because it contributes to something larger than yourself. Every person receives different gifts and opportunities, and each life unfolds differently. Instead of worrying about how you measure up to others, you can focus on being faithful with what God has entrusted to you.

Purpose is discovered through steady obedience. As you learn to work faithfully in the present, you will grow in wisdom and readiness for what lies ahead.

## Conversation Points

- How is purpose different from ambition?
- Why does faithfulness in small tasks matter?
- How can gifts be used for service rather than status?

# WEEK 11: IDENTITY IN CHRIST

*Father's Reflection*

In Christ, a man is redeemed and adopted into God's family. Achievements fluctuate, praise from others rises and falls, and recognition comes and goes. If a young man bases his identity on these shifting foundations, he becomes unstable, constantly chasing approval from what is temporary and often fleeting. He may feel elated when praised and dejected when overlooked. This kind of self-understanding leaves him vulnerable to pride, envy, and discouragement. As a father, you must ground both yourself and your son in a firmer reality, one that does not depend on external validation or momentary success. Union with Christ defines the believer. Acceptance before God rests not on performance or accomplishment, but entirely on grace. This foundation produces neither passivity nor complacency; it produces gratitude-driven obedience.

A father must repeatedly model this truth. When successes come, remind your son that accomplishment does not increase his value before God. When failures occur, remind him that setbacks do not remove him from God's care. The constancy of Christ steadies both moments. Identity in Christ fosters humility without insecurity and confidence without arrogance. It teaches that worth is inherent, not contingent.

It is also crucial to distinguish between fleeting emotions and true identity. Approval, recognition, and even personal talent are gifts and tools, not measures of worth. A man's true measure lies not in his accolades, popularity, or skill, but in his rootedness in Christ. Grace, rather than outcome, becomes the standard.

Fathers should strive to teach their sons that belonging precedes achievement. Security in Christ shapes how he engages the world: decisions, relationships, and leadership flow from this settled identity. A young man secure in Christ can act rightly without fear of losing value or relevance. He is freed to pursue responsibility, courage, and integrity, knowing that his ultimate worth is unshakable. Identity in Christ stabilizes character, anchors moral courage, and provides resilience in times of trial. It is the bedrock upon which true manhood is formed.

*Scripture*

## 📖 2 Corinthians 5:16–21 (ESV)

From now on, therefore, we regard no one according to the flesh. Even though we once regarded Christ according to the flesh, we regard him thus no longer. Therefore, if anyone is in Christ, he is a new creation. The old has passed away; behold, the new has come. All this is from God, who through Christ reconciled us to himself and gave us the ministry of reconciliation; that is, in Christ God was reconciling the world to himself, not counting their trespasses against them, and entrusting to us the message of reconciliation. Therefore, we are ambassadors for Christ, God making his appeal through us. We implore you on behalf of Christ, be reconciled to God. For our sake he made him to be sin who knew no sin, so that in him we might become the righteousness of God.

*Son's Reflection*

Many people build their identity on things that shift constantly, such as popularity, achievements, or the opinions of others. When those things change, their confidence changes with them. Identity in Christ is different. When you trust in Him, your value is not determined by your latest success or failure. God's acceptance does not depend on your performance. This allows you to pursue growth and responsibility without the constant fear of losing your worth.

This kind of security helps a young man remain steady. Success becomes something to be grateful for rather than something that defines him. Failure becomes an opportunity to learn rather than a reason to give up. Confidence grows because it is anchored in God rather than in temporary outcomes.

Knowing who you are in Christ also encourages humility. Your abilities and opportunities are gifts from God, not reasons to boast. At the same time, it gives courage. When you know that your identity is secure, you can do the right thing even when it is difficult or unpopular. Instead of constantly trying to earn approval, you begin to live out of the acceptance God has already given.

*Conversation Points*

- Why is it dangerous to base identity on achievement?

- How does belonging to Christ change the way we handle success and failure?

- What does it mean to live from acceptance rather than constantly seeking it?

## WEEK 12: REJECTING FALSE MODELS

*Father's Reflection*

Every generation presents distorted models of manhood. Some celebrate dominance, others detachment. Many reward bravado while neglecting character. A father's role is to help his son discern these distortions clearly. Cultural models often elevate strength without restraint, confidence without humility, and influence without integrity. Scripture presents a different vision. Strength is governed by self-control. Courage is joined to compassion. Leadership is shaped by service.

A father should expose counterfeit models calmly and without mockery, contrasting them with biblical virtues. Faithfulness, patience, integrity, and self-control form the foundation of true manhood. These qualities are often quiet, unseen, and steady. A man who chases performance-based masculinity may achieve attention, but he risks exhaustion and instability. A man who pursues Christlike character grows steadily, reliably, and with enduring impact.

It is vital to teach that not every loud voice or flashy display deserves imitation. True manhood is measured not by outward appearance or applause but by inner formation shaped by the Spirit. Sons must learn to evaluate models carefully, to resist imitation of the worldly ideal, and to pursue what is lasting rather than impressive.

A father's example, patience, and repeated instruction create a safe space in which his son can reflect, compare, and choose wisely. Through modeling and discussion, a young man begins to internalize the traits that Scripture honors. He learns that restraint, integrity, and service define a mature, godly man.

*Scripture*

### 📖 Micah 6:6–8 (ESV)

"With what shall I come before the Lord, and bow myself before God on high? Shall I come before him with burnt offerings, with calves a year old? Will the Lord be pleased with thousands of rams, with ten thousands of rivers of oil? Shall I give my firstborn for my transgression, the fruit of my body for the sin of my soul? "He has told you, O man, what is

good; and what does the Lord require of you but to do justice,
and to love kindness, and to walk humbly with your God?

*Son's Reflection*

Some people believe that strength means being aggressive or dominating others. Others think manhood is about popularity, appearance, or constant success. Scripture paints a different picture. True strength is connected to self-control, humility, and responsibility. A man who walks with God learns that courage and compassion belong together.

Real leadership is not about showing off power but about serving others faithfully.

When you can see the difference between what the world celebrates and what God values, it becomes easier to choose the right path. Humility plays a key role in this process. A humble man is willing to listen, learn, and grow. He does not need to prove his strength constantly because his confidence rests in God.

Choosing the example of Christ protects your judgment and shapes your actions. Over time, patience, integrity, and self-control become part of who you are. These qualities may not always attract attention, but they form the kind of strength that lasts.

*Conversation Points*

- What messages about manhood are most common in our culture?
- How do these differ from Scripture's description?
- Why is humility essential to true strength?

## WEEK 13: CHARACTER OVER PERFORMANCE

*Father's Reflection*

Performance may attract attention, but character sustains influence. A father must consistently communicate to his son that Christlike character matters far more than outward success, accolades, or visible achievement. The fruit of the Spirit (love, joy, peace, patience, kindness, goodness, faithfulness, gentleness, and self-control) reveals true maturity far more reliably than any display of skill, recognition, or temporary triumph. A man may appear strong, skilled, or accomplished, yet without the fruit of the Spirit, his influence is brittle and fleeting. True manhood is revealed not in isolated victories or dramatic moments, but in consistent choices. Steadiness in obedience, diligence in responsibility, and faithfulness in relationships demonstrate maturity more than performance ever could.

A father's patient example communicates that repeated practice, steady correction, and faithful discipline cultivate character over time. Sons need to see that enduring growth is not achieved through occasional effort or dramatic displays, but through daily commitment to what is right and good.

Character is built quietly and intentionally. Integrity exercised when no one is watching. Patience maintained in frustration. Love expressed through action rather than words. Self-control practiced under pressure. Humility upheld in moments of success. These traits do not make headlines, but they shape influence that endures. A father should model them visibly, admit mistakes, demonstrate repentance, and show that spiritual and moral growth is an ongoing process. Sons learn as much from what is lived and practiced as from what is taught in words.

By emphasizing Christlike character over performance, a father equips his son for lasting influence, faithful leadership, and a measure of manhood that is grounded in Scripture. What is applauded by the world fades; what is cultivated by the Spirit endures.

*Scripture*

### 📖 Galatians 5:16–24 (ESV)

> But I say, walk by the Spirit, and you will not gratify the desires of the flesh. For the desires of the flesh are against the Spirit, and the desires of the Spirit are against the flesh, for these are

opposed to each other, to keep you from doing the things you want to do. But if you are led by the Spirit, you are not under the law. Now the works of the flesh are evident: sexual immorality, impurity, sensuality, idolatry, sorcery, enmity, strife, jealousy, fits of anger, rivalries, dissensions, divisions, envy, drunkenness, orgies, and things like these. I warn you, as I warned you before, that those who do such things will not inherit the kingdom of God. But the fruit of the Spirit is love, joy, peace, patience, kindness, goodness, faithfulness, gentleness, self-control; against such things there is no law. And those who belong to Christ Jesus have crucified the flesh with its passions and desires.

## Son's Reflection

Achievements can be impressive, but they do not define a man. An achievement can attract attention for a moment, but it is character that determines the kind of influence a man will have over time. The Bible describes character through the fruit of the Spirit: love, joy, peace, patience, kindness, goodness, faithfulness, gentleness, and self-control. These qualities develop slowly as a person learns to follow God and make wise choices day after day.

When you focus on character rather than achievements, success and failure begin to look different. Success becomes an opportunity to show gratitude and humility. Failure becomes a chance to learn and grow rather than something that defines you. A young man who pursues character builds a foundation that lasts far longer than recognition or applause.

## Conversation Points

- Why does character matter more than performance?
- How does the fruit of the Spirit shape true manhood?
- What habits help cultivate integrity over time?

## What We're Building in These Weeks

A young man who sees his father model faithfulness, humility, and steadiness before God learns more than doctrine. He sees life formed in practice. Manhood begins with identity, not achievement. Every man is made in the image of God. A son who sees his father embracing calling as service, not competition, learns to value obedience over recognition. Identity in Christ provides stability. Grounded in this reality, a man grows in humility without insecurity and confidence without arrogance. Achievements may fade, but steady obedience and the fruit of the Spirit endure. True manhood is revealed in consistent choices shaped by Scripture, faith, and the quiet work of God.

By understanding who he is before God, a young man becomes resilient against the shifting definitions of the world. He will pursue strength with restraint, influence with integrity, and leadership with humility. Christlike manhood grows steadily, faithfully, and over time.

# Part Two:
## Strengthening Discipline and Stewardship



These weeks focus on doing the quiet work of building a strong and steady character. It is a reminder to fathers and sons alike that real strength comes from the patient mastery of self. Discipline, perseverance, and faithful effort are not burdens to endure but ways to live out obedience and worship. Ordinary life can become the clay God uses to build lasting strength, courage, and character.

♫ Scan to listen to "Hold the Line"

# CHAPTER 4

# Strength Under Restraint: Developing Self-Control

A man who cannot rule his own spirit is unprepared to lead others. True strength comes from self-mastery and forms the foundation of enduring character. Self-control is not a personality trait, and it is not achieved through a feat of willpower. It is the fruit of submission to God's authority. Identity precedes action. A man who belongs to Christ is no longer enslaved to the flesh. Sons must learn early that emotions are real but not sovereign. , and it is not achieved through a feat of submission to God's authority. Identity precedes action. A man who belongs to Christ is no longer enslaved to the flesh. Sons must learn early that emotions are real but not sovereign.

The guiding question for these weeks is both simple and searching: What does God want me to do right now?

## WEEK 14: KNOWING THE STRUGGLE

*Father's Reflection*

Self-control begins with honest recognition. A man cannot govern what he refuses to acknowledge. Scripture does not deny the presence of strong desires, emotional reactions, or inward conflict, but it calls believers to bring every part of their hearts under the authority of God's Word. Disciplined strength begins when a father acknowledges his own struggles without excuse or self-condemnation. Because we belong to Christ, we are no longer ruled by impulse. Purpose flows from belonging.

Emotions in themselves are not sinful. Anger, desire, frustration, and disappointment are part of living in a fallen world. Yet unchecked emotion can become a master. A raised voice, a harsh reply, a private indulgence, or a defensive posture often begins long before any outward action. It starts with unexamined triggers. Reflective restraint allows a man to notice these triggers and respond wisely. A father might model this to his son by taking a moment to pause when irritation arises. He might say, "I feel frustrated, but I must guide you with my words." This transparency teaches that strength is measured, deliberate, and guided by obedience rather than performance. Obedience is submitting to God's will, not proving oneself.

This week, fathers can guide sons to identify common triggers. What situations provoke impatience? What words stir defensiveness? What desires lead to compromise? Patterns may include conflict with siblings, online distractions, competitive pride, or sensitivity to criticism. Naming these struggles weakens their power.

Self-mastery is a foundational virtue. Leadership without self-control risks tyranny. Confidence without restraint risks arrogance. True strength listens before it reacts and reflects before it responds. A man who understands his inner battles is better prepared to submit willingly to God's Word rather than surrender to impulse.

*Scripture*

📖 **James 1:14–20 (ESV)**

> But each person is tempted when he is lured and enticed by his own desire. Then desire when it has conceived gives birth to sin, and sin when it is fully grown brings forth death.

Do not be deceived, my beloved brothers. Every good gift and every perfect gift is from above, coming down from the Father of lights, with whom there is no variation or shadow due to change. Of his own will he brought us forth by the word of truth, that we should be a kind of firstfruits of his creatures. Know this, my beloved brothers: let every person be quick to hear, slow to speak, slow to anger; for the anger of man does not produce the righteousness of God.

## Son's Reflection

Everyone experiences strong emotions. The Bible does not say that feeling anger, frustration, or desire is wrong. What matters is what you do next. Temptation often starts in your heart. A thought or desire grows, and if you act without thinking, it can lead to sin. That is why reflection is important. What usually sets you off? Is it criticism, losing a game, being told no, or seeing someone take advantage of you? Knowing your triggers helps you prepare and respond wisely.

Strength is not about reacting quickly. True strength is choosing well. When you feel a strong emotion rising, pause and ask, "What does God want me to do right now?" That question helps you focus on what really matters, rather than just your feelings.

God has given you a new identity in Christ. You are not controlled by your emotions. You can learn to be quick to listen, slow to speak, and slow to anger. Strong men reflect before they act. Each time you pause and choose what honors God, you grow in self-control, build character, and live in the freedom of your identity in Christ.

## Conversation Points

- What situations most often trigger strong emotions in you?

- How can recognizing a trigger help you respond differently next time?

- How does remembering your identity in Christ help you resist impulse?

## WEEK 15: PAUSE AND PRAY

*Father's Reflection*

Identifying a struggle does not guarantee transformation. Discipline must follow awareness. Scripture consistently calls men to active dependence on God. Controlled strength requires a deliberate interruption of impulse. The pause is not a sign of weakness; it is an act of submission.

Practically, this may look like stepping aside before continuing a tense conversation, or saying, "Let me think about that," rather than responding defensively. Fathers should model visible reliance on God. A simple prayer, such as " "Lord, give me wisdom," spoken aloud, demonstrates that true strength does not depend on personal willpower. The pause retrains the heart. It shifts the question from "How do I win this moment?" to "How do I honor God in this moment?" The book of Proverbs repeatedly links wisdom with restraint. A controlled spirit is far better than raw power.

Teaching sons to pause fosters humility. It reminds them that they are not self-sufficient and helps establish habits of prayer in the very moments when the flesh would otherwise rule. With time and repetition, the pause becomes instinctive. A man who pauses before acting acknowledges that God's authority governs his tongue, his temper, and his decisions. That acknowledgment is a quiet mark of maturity and a visible expression of strength.

*Scripture*

### 📖 Proverbs 16:28–33 (ESV)

A dishonest man spreads strife, and a whisperer separates close friends. A man of violence entices his neighbor and leads him in a way that is not good. Whoever winks his eyes plans dishonest things; he who purses his lips brings evil to pass. Gray hair is a crown of glory; it is gained in a righteous life. Whoever is slow to anger is better than the mighty, and he who rules his spirit than he who takes a city. The lot is cast into the lap, but its every decision is from the Lord.

*Son's Reflection*

Sometimes the biggest battles happen in just a few seconds. Someone says something unfair. A rule feels frustrating. You want to respond right away. In those moments, you have a choice. Before you speak or act, pause. Take a slow breath. Count to 10. Or pray a short prayer, such as, "Lord, help me choose what is right." That pause gives you time to think. Instead of reacting from emotion, you can ask, "What does God want me to do?" Maybe it means staying quiet. Maybe it means answering respectfully. Maybe it means walking away for a moment.10. Or pray a short prayer, such as, "Lord, help me choose what is right." That pause gives you time to think. Instead of reacting from emotion, you can ask, "What does God want me to do?" Maybe it means staying quiet. Maybe it means answering respectfully. Maybe it means walking away for a moment.

You will not always feel calm immediately. That is normal. You do not have to follow every feeling. Because you belong to Christ, you can rely on His help. Each time you pause and pray, you are training your heart. Over time, you will notice that you respond more wisely. That is strength growing under restraint, and it is how God builds true self-control in your life.

*Conversation Points*

- What usually makes it hardest for you to pause before reacting?

- What short prayer could you use in moments of tension?

- How can I model the practice of pausing better for you?

# WEEK 16: CHOOSING ACTION OVER IMPULSE

## Father's Reflection

It is not enough for a man to suppress a reaction; he must replace impulse with obedience. Scripture consistently calls men to walk by the Spirit, actively choosing what is right rather than simply restraining what is wrong. Strength becomes visible when a father chooses what honors God rather than what satisfies immediate desire. Like a compass needle, the magnetic pull of impulse can steer a man toward what feels comfortable in the moment. Obedience redirects that pull, aligning his thoughts and actions with God's Word.

A man who belongs to Christ is no longer governed by shifting appetites. His decisions should reflect submission to divine authority. When irritated, he chooses measured correction rather than harshness. These are not dramatic gestures, yet they form the framework of Christlike character. This discipline requires honest evaluation of one's motives. Is this choice driven by comfort, pride, fear, or convenience? Or is it driven by conviction and obedience to God?

Sons must be trained to slow the decision-making process and consider the consequences of their actions. A practical habit is asking three questions before acting: Does this honor God? Does this strengthen my character? Does this serve others?

The flesh seeks immediate gratification, but the Spirit produces enduring fruit. Every choice strengthens one influence or the other. When a father models deliberate obedience, he teaches his son that true strength is measured, thoughtful, and anchored in submission to God's Word.

## Scripture

### 📖 Proverbs 4:20–27 (ESV)

My son, be attentive to my words; incline your ear to my sayings. Let them not escape from your sight; keep them within your heart. For they are life to those who find them, and healing to all their flesh. Keep your heart with all vigilance, for from it flow the springs of life. Put away from you crooked speech, and put devious talk far from you. Let your eyes look directly forward, and your gaze be straight before you. Ponder the path of your feet; then all your ways will be sure. Do not swerve to the right or to the left; turn your foot away from evil.

*Son's Reflection*

Often, the hardest part of being a godly man is choosing what is right instead of what feels easy. You may want to argue back, quit something difficult, look at something you should avoid, or ignore a responsibility. Being godly means asking a better question than "What do I want?" It means asking, "What is the right thing to do?", the hardest part of being a godly man is choosing what is right instead of what feels easy. You may want to argue back, quit something difficult, look at something you should avoid, or ignore a responsibility. Being godly means asking a better question than "What do I want?" It means asking, "What is the right thing to do?"

The Bible teaches that the flesh and the Spirit pull in different directions. If you follow every impulse, you will form habits that weaken you. But if you walk by the Spirit, you grow stronger inside. Each right choice, even a small one, trains your heart. You will not always feel like doing what honors God, and that is normal. Strength means choosing obedience anyway. These choices shape who you become.

When you pause and choose what is right, you are building character. That is real strength. That is how purpose flows from belonging to Christ. Each time you choose the Spirit over impulse, you are learning to live as a man guided by God's Word.

*Conversation Points*

- What recent situation required you to choose between impulse and obedience?

- What makes it difficult to choose what is right in the moment?

- How can asking "What does God want me to do?" change your response?

# WEEK 17: CALM IN CONFLICT

*Father's Reflection*

Conflict reveals the depths of a man's self-control. Anyone can appear composed when circumstances are favorable, but strength is proven when challenges arise. Scripture consistently teaches us that wisdom is marked by measured speech and patient listening. A father who remains calm under pressure models composure, but more importantly, he demonstrates submission to God's authority over his tongue and temper. Anger itself is not always sinful, but uncontrolled anger produces harm. A father who is secure in his identity in Christ does not need to win every argument. His goal is not to pursue dominance, but righteousness. Fathers must model this, especially within the home.us that wisdom is marked by measured speech and patient listening. A father who remains calm under pressure models composure, but more importantly, he demonstrates submission to God's authority over his tongue and temper. Anger itself is not always sinful, but uncontrolled anger produces harm. A father who is secure in his identity in Christ does not need to win every argument. His goal is not to pursue dominance, but righteousness. Fathers must model this, especially within the home.

When a son speaks sharply, the natural impulse is to respond with force or authority. Yet strength may require responding quietly. When disagreement arises between siblings, a father can guide the discussion rather than impose an immediate verdict. This demonstrates that leadership includes patience and discernment.the discussion rather than impose an immediate verdict. This demonstrates that leadership includes patience and discernment.

A controlled spirit reduces escalation and invites resolution. A man who can remain composed when challenged is fit to lead because he is not mastered by emotion. Calm in conflict is not passive tolerance. It is active restraint guided by wisdom. Calmness requires humility. Pride fuels defensiveness, and insecurity demands victory. A Christlike character seeks truth and peace. Submission to God's Word governs not only what is said, but how it is said.A Christlike character seeks truth and peace. Submission to God's Word governs not only what is said, but how it is said.

*Scripture*

## 📖 Proverbs 15:1–5 (ESV)

A soft answer turns away wrath, but a harsh word stirs up anger. The tongue of the wise commends knowledge, but the mouths of fools pour out folly. The eyes of the Lord are in every place, keeping watch on the evil and the good. A gentle tongue is a tree of life, but perverseness in it breaks the spirit. A fool despises his father's instruction, but whoever heeds reproof is prudent.

*Son's Reflection*

Conflict is a part of life. Someone misunderstands you or says something unfair. You feel the urge to defend yourself immediately. The Bible says to be quick to listen and slow to speak. That means strength begins with listening. When you interrupt or raise your voice, conflict grows. When you listen fully and answer calmly, tension often decreases.

Staying calm does not mean pretending nothing is wrong. It means choosing self-control. You can lower your voice. You can pause before answering. You can ask, "Can you explain what you mean?" These actions show maturity.

When you belong to Christ, you do not have to win every argument. Your identity is secure. Because of that, you can focus on responding in a way that honors God. Each time you choose composure over reaction, you are growing.

*Conversation Points*

- How can listening fully change the outcome of disagreement?

- Why does security in Christ reduce the need to "win" arguments?

- What practical steps can we practice as a family to handle conflict calmly?

## What We're Building in These Weeks

A father and son who learn self-control are submitting their inner lives to God's authority. They recognize the struggles within, pause and pray before acting, choose righteousness over immediate satisfaction, and remain calm when challenged. Each discipline builds on the others. Awareness prepares the mind. The pause cultivates dependence on God. Choosing obedience over impulse strengthens the heart.

Self-control is foundational to leadership. Without it, strength can become destructive. With it, strength becomes protective, steady, and trustworthy. Fathers are called to model visible reliance on God. Sons are called to internalize the question, "What does God want me to do?" When that question governs thought and action, a life marked by measured speech, disciplined desire, and steady obedience is formed.

Controlled strength equips a man to lead with integrity, serve with humility, and endure with faithfulness. It trains him to respond rather than react, to guide rather than dominate, and to act according to God's Word rather than his impulses. This kind of strength is quiet, consistent, and lasting, forming the foundation for a life of Christlike character.

# CHAPTER 5

# Endurance Over Comfort: Building Habitual Courage

Perseverance is the cornerstone of courage. A man's life is not measured by ease or visible success, but by faithful endurance. He endures because he serves a faithful God. Biblical courage is not loud bravado; it is holding firmly to God's promises when circumstances test resolve.

Fathers play a central role in forming this endurance. Sons must learn early that godliness is not built on dramatic spiritual experiences alone. It is shaped in ordinary days through steady obedience. Choosing endurance over comfort prepares a man to stand firm when greater trials come. What begins as small faithfulness becomes resilient character.

## WEEK 18: SMALL STEPS, BIG IMPACT

*Father's Reflection*

Perseverance is not forged in extraordinary moments alone. It is established in the near-invisible patterns of daily obedience. Scripture consistently teaches us that faithfulness in small matters precedes stewardship of greater responsibility. A father who desires to shape courage in his son must begin here. Identity precedes action. Because a man belongs to Christ, his daily habits are not attempts to earn favor but expressions of submission to God's Word.

Large trials do not create character; they reveal it. What a man repeatedly practices in private becomes visible under pressure. Therefore, the ordinary day becomes the training ground for endurance. A father models this when he orders his life under God's authority in quiet, consistent ways: rising early to pray before the household stirs, opening Scripture daily whether inclined or weary, completing work with diligence rather than complaint, and speaking with measured tone even in minor inconveniences. These practices may appear small, yet they establish spiritual stability.

Ten faithful minutes in the Word each morning shape the heart more deeply than occasional bursts of intensity followed by neglect. Ruling oneself includes ruling one's schedule. When a father guards time for prayer, fulfills commitments without excuse, and honors responsibilities before seeking leisure, he shows that obedience over performance governs his life. Growth and discipline must remain united. A father should speak openly with his son about the battle against distraction, fatigue, and apathy, showing that perseverance involves humility. At the same time, he should establish tangible practices: shared devotional time, weekly review of responsibilities, and clear expectations regarding follow-through. What begins as unnoticed faithfulness matures into resilient character fit for leadership.

*Scripture*

### 📖 Luke 16:10–13 (ESV)

One who is faithful in a very little is also faithful in much, and one who is dishonest in a very little is also dishonest in much. If then you have not been faithful in the unrighteous wealth, who will entrust to you the true riches? And if you have not been faithful in that which is another's, who will give you that which is your own? No servant can serve two masters, for either he will hate the one and love the other, or he will be devoted to the one and despise the other. You cannot serve God and money.

*Son's Reflection*

Most growth does not feel dramatic. You may not feel different after reading the Bible for 10 minutes. You may not feel brave when you finish your chores or pray before school. But those small choices matter more than you think.

Jesus teaches that faithfulness in little things prepares you for greater things. That means what you do in ordinary moments shapes who you become. Obedience is not about mood. It is about commitment. Some days you will feel motivated. Other days you will not. Identity precedes action. Because you belong to Christ, you obey Him whether you feel inspired or not.

Start with simple steps. Choose a consistent time to read Scripture. Pray briefly but sincerely. Complete responsibilities without needing reminders. When you practice these habits daily, you build trust in yourself and in God's help. Over time, you will notice that you can follow through even when it is difficult. Courage does not begin in crisis. It begins in routine. Each small act of obedience strengthens your character.

*Conversation Points*

- What small daily habit would most strengthen your spiritual life right now?

- Why is consistency more important than intensity?

- What makes it difficult to maintain simple routines?

## WEEK 19: RISING TO CHALLENGES

*Father's Reflection*

While routine forms the foundation of endurance, growth requires increasing responsibility. Scripture presents maturity as progressive strengthening. God does not leave His people stagnant; He refines them through measured difficulty. A father must therefore guide his son into challenges that stretch resolve without crushing spirit.

Endurance develops when discomfort is faced rather than avoided. Identity precedes action: A son belongs to Christ before he proves himself. Therefore, challenges are not tests of worth but instruments of growth. A father should frame difficulty accordingly. When assigning extended responsibilities, he is not imposing burden. Rather, he is cultivating perseverance.

Practical training matters. Encourage disciplined physical effort that requires sustained focus. Guide him through difficult conversations, teaching respectful speech under tension. Allow him to experience the weight of follow-through when tasks extend beyond immediate gratification. Walk beside him without removing every obstacle. In doing so, you as a father are demonstrating that obedience over performance shapes true courage. Speak openly about fear, frustration, and the temptation to quit. Teach your son that unease does not signal retreat. Scripture reminds us that trials produce steadfastness. A father who remains calm during his son's struggle communicates that growth often feels uncomfortable. Patience under strain becomes visible instruction.

Gradual exposure to challenge prepares a son for adulthood, where responsibilities multiply, and pressures intensify. Avoiding discomfort weakens resolve. Facing it wisely strengthens it. When a father models perseverance in his own work, service, and leadership, he reinforces the fact that submission to God's Word governs both private effort and public responsibility. Courage matures when a young man repeatedly chooses faithfulness over ease.

*Scripture*

### 📖 James 1:12–15 (ESV)

Blessed is the man who remains steadfast under trial, for when
he has stood the test he will receive the crown of life, which

God has promised to those who love him. Let no one say when he is tempted, "I am being tempted by God," for God cannot be tempted with evil, and he himself tempts no one. But each person is tempted when he is lured and enticed by his own desire. Then desire when it has conceived gives birth to sin, and sin when it is fully grown brings forth death.

## Son's Reflection

Some challenges feel uncomfortable at first. A hard assignment. A difficult conversation. A responsibility that stretches you. Your first reaction may be to avoid it or delay it. That response is natural, but it does not produce growth. The Bible teaches that trials produce steadfastness. This means God uses difficulty to strengthen your faith and shape your character.

You do not have to solve everything at once. Break the challenge into smaller, manageable steps. Stay calm. Focus on the next faithful action rather than the entire outcome. Ask yourself, "What is the right thing to do right now?" Obedience over performance keeps you grounded. Your goal is not to impress others but to remain faithful to Christ in each step.

When you complete something difficult, even imperfectly, your confidence grows. You begin to see that discomfort does not control you. Identity precedes action—you belong to Christ before you succeed. Because of that, you can face challenges without fear of failure defining you. God is forming endurance in you. Courage grows each time you choose to continue rather than quit.

## Conversation Points

- What recent challenge required you to persevere?
- How did breaking the task into smaller steps help you stay steady?
- What thoughts make you want to quit when something feels difficult?
- How can remembering your identity in Christ strengthen you during challenges?

# WEEK 20: HABITUAL FAITH

*Father's Reflection*

Scripture portrays godliness as a life of repeated, faithful action rather than a series of dramatic feats. Endurance is a way of life, not a single event. Because a man belongs to Christ, his choices are governed by loyalty to God rather than fleeting feelings. Identity precedes action. His belonging gives meaning to daily faithfulness and steadies him when emotion fluctuates.

A father must do what is right even when it goes unnoticed or feels inconvenient. Reading Scripture at a consistent time each day, praying without seeking recognition, serving family members without expectation of reward, and completing responsibilities diligently are not extraordinary acts. Yet repeated faithfully, they train the will and fortify character. Submission to God's Word is demonstrated not only in public leadership but in private consistency. The repetition of faithful choices produces resilience that will endure larger trials.

Courage is not the absence of fear or difficulty. It is the repeated decision to obey when obedience is costly or uncomfortable. A father should explain that obedience over performance governs the Christian life. We act faithfully not to earn approval but because we already belong to Christ. Sons must be guided to recognize that faithful actions, however small, matter in God's sight. Quiet perseverance should be affirmed without creating pride. Celebrate steady effort rather than visible success. Emphasize growth in character rather than outward achievement. In doing so, a father reinforces that purpose flows from belonging and that Christlike character is shaped through repetition.

As faith matures, it forms a man who is not dependent on comfort, immediate results, or applause. He learns to approach difficult situations with steadiness because his confidence rests in God's authority. Courage becomes the byproduct of obedience. Habitual faith is endurance made visible in daily submission. It is the bedrock upon which lasting leadership and godly manhood are built.

*Scripture*

### 📖 Hebrews 12: 6–10 (ESV)

"My son, do not regard lightly the discipline of the Lord, nor
be weary when reproved by him. For the Lord disciplines the

one he loves, and chastises every son whom he receives."It is for discipline that you have to endure. God is treating you as sons. For what son is there whom his father does not discipline? If you are left without discipline, in which all have participated, then you are illegitimate children and not sons. Besides this, we have had earthly fathers who disciplined us and we respected them. Shall we not much more be subject to the Father of spirits and live? For they disciplined us for a short time as it seemed best to them, but he disciplines us for our good, that we may share his holiness.

*Son's Reflection*

Courage is doing the right thing again and again. It is not only one big moment of bravery. Reading God's Word, completing responsibilities, and praying may seem ordinary. You may not feel bold while doing them. You may not see immediate results. Yet Scripture teaches that repeated obedience builds strength over time. Because you belong to Christ, you obey Him even when you do not feel motivated. Each small act of faithfulness prepares you for the next challenge.

When something feels hard or uncomfortable, habitual faith reminds you to keep going. You do not quit simply because it is difficult. Instead, you take the next faithful step. Those small, steady choices build confidence. You begin to see that God helps you follow through. Courage is doing what is right even when no one is watching. Private obedience shapes public character. Every time you endure instead of giving up, your heart grows stronger. Each faithful step matters because it forms who you are becoming.

*Conversation Points*

- How do repeated small acts of obedience prepare you for bigger challenges?

- Why is private faithfulness just as important as public success?

- When are you most tempted to quit, and why?

- What practical step can you take this week to build a consistent habit of obedience?

# WEEK 21: STEADFAST ENCOURAGEMENT

*Father's Reflection*

The value of encouragement and gentle guidance cannot be overstated. A father's consistent presence is a powerful instrument in forming courage within his son. Scripture repeatedly affirms that endurance grows not only through personal effort but also through faithful support within godly relationships. God often strengthens His people through the steady influence of others who exhort, correct, and walk beside them.

Endurance matures best in an atmosphere of patient accountability. A father who corrects without harshness and affirms without flattery reflects Christlike strength. Encouragement that is not conditioned upon visible success teaches a son that obedience over performance governs the Christian life. When approval is tied only to outcomes, perseverance weakens. When affirmation highlights faithfulness, effort, and submission to God's Word, endurance deepens.

A father shapes courage by asking thoughtful questions about habits, attitudes, and motives. He models composure in difficulty. He admits his own need for grace. He demonstrates perseverance in work, service, and spiritual discipline. These practices reveal that identity precedes action. A son learns that he belongs to Christ before he achieves anything of note. That belonging becomes the foundation for continued effort. Presence is essential. By remaining attentive and engaged, a father communicates that perseverance is not a solitary pursuit. God supplies sustaining grace, and a father's faithful involvement reinforces reliance upon that grace. Gentle accountability unlocks endurance more effectively than pressure or criticism. Correction should direct the heart back to submission to God's authority rather than merely adjusting behavior.

Steadfast encouragement creates a culture of resilience within the home. Sons learn that daily obedience matters more than occasional displays of strength. Courage is reinforced through consistency, patience, and relational investment. A father who teaches through presence, calm instruction, and quiet support equips his son with endurance that will remain long after temporary discomfort has faded.

*Scripture*

📖 **1 Thessalonians 5:5–11 (ESV)**

For you are all children of light, children of the day. We are not of the night or of the darkness. So then let us not sleep, as others do, but let us keep awake and be sober. For those who sleep, sleep at night, and those who get drunk, are drunk at night. But since we belong to the day, let us be sober, having put on the breastplate of faith and love, and for a helmet the hope of salvation. For God has not destined us for wrath, but to obtain salvation through our Lord Jesus Christ, who died for us so that whether we are awake or asleep we might live with him. Therefore encourage one another and build one another up, just as you are doing.

*Son's Reflection*

Having someone steady beside you makes a real difference. Courage grows more steadily when your father shows up consistently, encourages you, and guides you without demanding perfection. God values faithfulness more than impressive results. That means what matters most is not how dramatic your success looks, but whether you continue in obedience. You belong to Christ before you accomplish anything. Because of that, you do not have to prove your worth. You are learning to live out who you already are.

You will not do everything perfectly, as there are bound to be setbacks. However, courage grows through repeated choices to keep going. When your father notices your effort and consistency, not just outcomes, you learn that obedience over performance shapes real strength. Encouragement helps you see that growth takes time.

Endurance is built slowly. Each day you practice. Each time you finish a hard task. Each moment you choose not to quit. These decisions form Christlike character. This kind of courage does not disappear when circumstances change. It lasts because it is rooted in faithfulness.

*Conversation Points*

- How does steady encouragement help you persevere when something feels difficult?
- When do you feel pressure to perform instead of simply being faithful?

- How can we encourage effort and consistency in our home?

- What practical step can we take this week to support one another in daily perseverance?

## What We're Building in These Weeks

Faith teaches us that enduring discomfort, completing necessary responsibilities, and facing challenges with composure are essential elements of godly courage. Perseverance is not accidental. It is formed through steady obedience and submission to God's Word. A man does not endure in order to earn belonging. He endures because he belongs to Christ. Courage matures when faithfulness is repeated in ordinary moments.

Steadfast encouragement from a father reinforces the notion that perseverance is not solitary. God provides sustaining grace, and a father's presence, patience, and relational investment strengthen a son's resolve. In this environment, sons learn to value quiet consistency above attention or applause. They see that leadership begins with self-government and that strength is expressed through restraint, humility, and loyalty to Christ.

True courage is learned daily, practiced consistently, and sustained by grace. What is built here is not a temporary resolve, but enduring faithfulness fit for lifelong discipleship.

# CHAPTER 6

# Stewardship of Time and Work: Honoring God in Daily Life

Work and time are gifts from God, entrusted to every man for service, growth, and worship. Scripture portrays work as both a responsibility and a reflection of God's character. Genesis 2 shows us that God placed Adam in the garden to care for it, demonstrating that labor itself is part of His good design. Likewise, the Sabbath emphasizes that rest is not laziness but trust in God's provision and acknowledgment of His sovereignty. Daily routines and intentional work are acts of worship. Every chore completed faithfully, every task done with care, and every assignment approached with diligence honors God.

## WEEK 22: REST AS TRUST

*Father's Reflection*

Rest is more than the absence of labor; it is a deliberate act of trust in God. A man belongs to God, not to the endless demands of work, ambition, or the pressures of productivity. Scripture portrays rest as an essential rhythm built into creation itself. God instituted work followed by pause, activity followed by reflection, demonstrating that life is sustained by His provision and not by human effort alone. Observing rest is a tangible acknowledgment that control and favor are not earned by constant action.

A father has the responsibility to model rest intentionally. This does not mean idleness, but rather a purposeful pause for worship, reflection, and meaningful family engagement. By intentionally setting aside time for Sabbath-like rest, a father teaches his son that true strength and endurance are rooted in dependence on God rather than relentless effort. Rest is an opportunity to demonstrate obedience to God's design, showing that withdrawal from labor is not weakness but wisdom applied in daily life. Identifying essential tasks and eliminating nonessential ones allows a day to focus on worship, Scripture reading, prayer, and family connection. Resting together provides opportunities for relational investment and spiritual instruction. Sons observe that God-given productivity is inseparable from deliberate rest, and that a life of obedience is structured with both effort and pause.

A man who honors rest consistently develops patience, steadiness of heart, and the ability to approach work without compulsion or anxiety. He trains himself and his household to recognize that obedience to God includes stewardship of time and energy. Sons learn that true trust manifests in the balance between work and rest, and that this balance is not incidental but a reflection of submission to God's authority.

*Scripture*

### 📖 Exodus 20:8–11 (ESV)

"Remember the Sabbath day, to keep it holy. Six days you shall labor, and do all your work, but the seventh day is a Sabbath to the Lord your God. On it you shall not do any work, you, or your son, or your daughter, your male servant, or your female servant, or your livestock, or the sojourner who is within your gates. For in six days the Lord made the heavens and the earth, the sea, and all that is in them, and rested on the seventh day. Therefore the Lord blessed the Sabbath day and made it holy.

*Son's Reflection*

Rest is not wasted time. Taking a day to pause, reflect, and worship is an act of trust in God. You do not have to prove yourself by being busy all the time. God provides for your needs, and choosing rest shows that you rely on Him instead of your own effort. Observing a Sabbath or a quiet day allows your mind, body, and spirit to recharge so you can serve faithfully.

Rest also teaches patience and perspective. When you stop striving constantly, you learn that life is not defined by activity or accomplishments. You see that God sustains you, and that your worth does not depend on what you can do. By participating in rest intentionally, you learn to honor His design for work and pause, understanding that both are necessary to live well.

Remember: True trust in God is defined by balancing effort with pause. Rest is not a break from responsibility; it is part of faithful living. When you rest well, you strengthen your body, your mind, and your heart for the work and challenges God calls you to.

*Conversation Points*

- Why do you think God commands rest as part of His law?

- How can taking a day of rest show trust in God?

- What routines could help make your rest intentional rather than accidental?

- How does resting well prepare you for faithful work?

# WEEK 23: INTENTIONAL RHYTHMS

*Father's Reflection*

Time is one of the most valuable resources God entrusts to a man. Without deliberate attention, hours can pass unnoticed, leaving little accomplished and much wasted. Scripture emphasizes the importance of ordering one's life wisely, and a father's example provides the clearest lesson in this principle. A man who belongs to Christ submits his schedule to God's authority. Every hour is an opportunity to honor Him, not a chance to follow whim or convenience. Intentional rhythms create a framework for faithfulness, teaching sons to integrate worship, study, work, and family responsibilities into their daily lives.

Purposeful routines do not limit freedom; they enable it. When sons see their father rise early for prayer, dedicate consistent time to Scripture, complete chores, engage in study, and participate in family interaction, they witness that order does not constrain life but structures it for effectiveness. Sons learn that planning is not about perfection but about prioritizing what is most important and resisting distraction. Fathers can reinforce this by creating simple, visible practices: a weekly schedule, designated times for devotion and study, reminders of household duties, and moments set aside for reflection and prayer.

Intentional rhythms also communicate a deeper lesson about stewardship. God values not only the tasks a man performs but also how he manages the time and energy to accomplish them. Teaching sons to approach each hour thoughtfully, to honor commitments promptly, and to treat interruptions and leisure with discernment instills endurance, discipline, and reliability. By demonstrating consistency and order, a father shows that Christlike character is expressed not only through visible achievements but also through faithful stewardship of life's ordinary moments. Sons who internalize this principle develop a foundation of self-control and discernment that prepares them for leadership, responsibility, and service that honors God.

A father who models intentional rhythms communicates that daily obedience and reflection are not burdens but opportunities to serve God and others faithfully. Time spent wisely fosters growth, steadiness, and confidence, establishing habits that carry sons into adulthood with purpose, resilience, and a clear understanding of the value of every hour.

*Scripture*

## 📖 Ecclesiastes 3:1–8 (ESV)

For everything there is a season, and a time for every matter under heaven: a time to be born, and a time to die; a time to plant, and a time to pluck up what is planted; a time to kill, and a time to heal; a time to break down, and a time to build up; a time to weep, and a time to laugh; a time to mourn, and a time to dance; a time to cast away stones, and a time to gather stones together; a time to embrace, and a time to refrain from embracing;a time to seek, and a time to lose; a time to keep, and a time to cast away; a time to tear, and a time to sew; a time to keep silence, and a time to speak; a time to love, and a time to hate; a time for war, and a time for peace.

*Son's Reflection*

God wants you to use your time with purpose, not just go from one thing to the next without direction. Daily routines help you live intentionally and show that every hour can be meaningful. Planning your day does not take away freedom. Instead, it helps you focus on what matters most and avoid wasting energy on distractions. When you know what comes next, you can complete work, study, and chores with attention and care.

Following simple rhythms builds habits that last. Doing the same things at predictable times trains your mind to focus, your heart to persevere, and your hands to work steadily. It also teaches responsibility, because you see the connection between your daily actions and the outcomes they produce. The small habits you repeat now prepare you for bigger responsibilities later.

God values how you spend your hours. Planning your day, completing tasks, and honoring commitments are all ways to serve Him. Using your time wisely strengthens your character, helps you grow in self-discipline, and trains you to be reliable. When you follow intentional rhythms, you honor God with your life, not just with what you do, but with how you manage the time He has given you.

*Conversation Points*

- What parts of your day are currently unstructured or inconsistent?

- How can daily routines help you focus better on God and responsibilities?

- How does seeing me plan my day help you understand intentional living?

# WEEK 24: GUARDING ATTENTION

## *Father's Reflection*

The value of time is measured not only in hours spent but in focus maintained. Scripture repeatedly calls men to serve God with undivided hearts, emphasizing that distraction diminishes both effectiveness and spiritual maturity. A father's role is to model attentive diligence, demonstrating to his son that every task, whether small or significant, requires deliberate engagement. Guarding attention is a practical exercise in obedience, patience, and discipline. It teaches that faithfulness extends beyond visible results to the integrity of effort.

A man who disciplines his mind and directs his focus shows his son how to honor God in every responsibility. This includes resisting the pull of screens, idle conversation, or unnecessary activity while engaged in work, study, or service. Fathers demonstrate this principle by giving full attention to their assigned tasks, speaking deliberately when teaching, and maintaining composure when minor interruptions arise. This way, sons learn that distractions are not harmless; they erode the capacity to complete work well and cultivate self-control. Sons should be taught to complete one task fully before moving to the next. Multitasking may appear efficient, but it divides effort and diminishes quality, weakening perseverance. Fathers can reinforce focus by pointing out moments when attention is maintained or lost, explaining the spiritual and practical consequences of divided effort.

Guarding attention is more than a technique; it is an expression of obedience. A man who approaches every chore, responsibility, or act of service with undistracted effort demonstrates that his actions have eternal significance because they honor God. Attention becomes a form of worship, training the heart to value the present moment, fulfill commitments faithfully, and steward time as a gift. Sons who witness and practice this principle develop the habits of discipline, diligence, and patience. They internalize that the quality of effort matters as much as the completion of the task.

By emphasizing focus as an act of obedience, a father equips his son to approach life with deliberate purpose. Every hour, every task, and every duty becomes an opportunity to exercise discipline, honor God, and build character that endures. The lessons learned through concentrated attention extend into work, relationships, study, and spiritual life, preparing a young man for leadership and faithful service.

## *Scripture*

### 📖 Luke 10:38–42 (ESV)

Now as they went on their way, Jesus entered a village. And a woman named Martha welcomed him into her house. And she had a sister called Mary, who sat at the Lord's feet and listened to his teaching. But Martha was distracted with much serving. And she went up to him and said, "Lord, do you not care that my sister has left me to serve alone? Tell her then to help me." But the Lord answered her, "Martha, Martha, you are anxious and troubled about many things, but one thing is necessary. Mary has chosen the good portion, which will not be taken away from her."

## *Son's Reflection*

Paying attention is a skill that grows with practice. God wants your heart and mind focused on what matters, not scattered across distractions. When you focus on one task at a time, you are learning discipline. Screens, noise, or rushing through things make it hard to give your best. By guarding your attention, you honor God in the work He gives you.

Fathers help by showing you how to concentrate and by creating spaces free from distraction. Following their example teaches patience, care, and diligence. In time, completing tasks with focus becomes a habit, not a chore. Your attention is a gift. Using it wisely strengthens your character, builds reliability, and trains your mind to serve God faithfully.

## *Conversation Points*

- What distracts you most when you are trying to focus?

- How can you structure your space or time to guard your attention?

- Why does focusing on one task at a time honor God?

- When you give full attention to a task, how does it feel compared to rushing or multitasking?

# WEEK 25: WORK AS WORSHIP

*Father's Reflection*

Work is not merely a necessity; it is a calling. From the simplest household task to complex responsibilities at work, every act can honor God when approached with care, thoughtfulness, and diligence. Sons observe not only the outcome of work but the manner in which it is done. They see whether a father labors with purpose or drifts through tasks without attention. In these moments, character is formed quietly, and the foundations of integrity are laid.

Effort and obedience become inseparable when you engage in every task faithfully. Pride, hurry, or carelessness communicates that work is merely functional. Sons absorb these lessons naturally as they witness their father's approach, seeing that God values faithfulness more than outward recognition.

Work is also a training ground for internal qualities. Patience grows when a task is completed thoroughly rather than rushed. Responsibility develops when a father allows a son to share in duties while guiding him toward careful execution. Thoughtfulness emerges when a father explains why a job matters, not for applause, but because diligence honors God and benefits others. Fathers can reinforce these lessons by providing opportunities for sons to engage meaningfully in work. Rather than simply telling a son to "do it right," a father can teach through demonstration, showing how to plan, prepare, and execute each task with care. Involving sons in routine responsibilities communicates that no work is insignificant when done for God's glory. Faithfulness in ordinary labor builds habits that endure into adulthood, shaping men capable of disciplined, dependable service in every sphere of life.

Approaching work as worship reshapes the heart and mind. Sons learn that every task is an opportunity to glorify God. A household that treats work in this way forms young men who understand that reliability, diligence, and thoughtful effort are marks of Christlike character.

*Scripture*

📖 **Proverbs 12: 24–28 (ESV)**

The hand of the diligent will rule, while the slothful will be put to forced labor. Anxiety in a man's heart weighs him down, but a good word makes him glad. One who is righteous is a guide to his neighbor, but the way of the wicked leads them astray. Whoever is slothful will not roast his game, but the diligent man will get precious wealth. In the path of righteousness is life, and in its pathway there is no death.

*Son's Reflection*

Work is not just something you have to do. Every task is a chance to honor God. How you do it matters more than how much you do or whether anyone notices. Doing your work carefully and with attention shows that you take God seriously and respect what He has given you.

It is easy to rush through tasks or do just enough to get by. But faithfulness means giving your best effort consistently, even when it seems small or unimportant. Completing a chore thoroughly, finishing a school assignment on time, or helping a family member without being asked trains your heart to serve with integrity. You are learning that diligence and obedience go together. Excellence is not about being perfect. It is about giving your best because God is watching. Each task you complete faithfully builds habits that strengthen your character, trains your discipline, and prepares you for larger responsibilities in life. When work is done this way, it becomes an act of worship, and courage, reliability, and trustworthiness grow naturally.

*Conversation Points*

- Which task could you approach this week with more care to honor God?

- How does seeing your father work diligently help you understand obedience in action?

- What changes when you focus on doing your work for God rather than for people?

# WEEK 26: DILIGENCE AND RELIABILITY

*Father's Reflection*

Consistency and reliability are at the heart of godly stewardship. Sons learn endurance, integrity, and character most effectively by watching their fathers follow through in daily responsibilities. Diligence is the steady application of effort, while reliability is the faithful completion of commitments. Both reflect identity in Christ, showing that a man's character is revealed in how he handles ordinary tasks. Purpose flows from belonging; a man who belongs to God approaches every responsibility with seriousness because it matters to Him.

Teaching diligence begins with example. A father demonstrates reliability through visible actions: completing household tasks conscientiously, honoring schedules without complaint, and meeting obligations with care. Practical instruction is equally important. Fathers can assign daily responsibilities, follow up with accountability, and provide guidance on planning and execution. These experiences teach sons that reliability is not innate but developed through repeated, faithful choices. A man who finishes a chore he does not want to do, turns in work on time, or responds promptly to commitments models the principle that integrity is cultivated through practice, not occasional display.

A young man must understand that diligence is not self-promotion. It is an expression of obedience and submission to God. Fathers should explain that rushing, cutting corners, or seeking applause undermines character, whereas patience, thoroughness, and quiet effort align labor with God's glory. Externally, accountability reinforces the lesson that reliability is relational; others can trust you because you consistently act with faithfulness.

As sons practice diligence and reliability, they develop confidence in their own abilities and a reputation for trustworthiness. These habits prepare them for greater responsibilities, leadership, and faithful service. Fathers who embody these virtues communicate that excellence in ordinary tasks reflects Christlike character and glorifies God. The integration of consistent effort, careful attention, and steadfast commitment forms men capable of honoring God in every area of life.

*Scripture*

## 📖 Lamentations 3:22–27 (ESV)

The steadfast love of the Lord never ceases; his mercies never come to an end; they are new every morning; great is your faithfulness. "The Lord is my portion," says my soul, "therefore I will hope in him." The Lord is good to those who wait for him, to the soul who seeks him. It is good that one should wait quietly for the salvation of the Lord. It is good for a man that he bear the yoke in his youth.

*Son's Reflection*

Being reliable means people can trust you to do what you say you will. When you follow through on chores, school assignments, or responsibilities at home, you show God and others that you take your duties seriously. Diligence is not about doing everything perfectly. It is about putting steady effort into every task, even when no one is watching.

Watching your father complete his responsibilities faithfully teaches an important lesson. You see that reliability is built over time and that character is formed in ordinary actions. When you practice finishing what you start and handling tasks carefully, you are learning to live faithfully in small things. These habits matter because they prepare you for bigger responsibilities and challenges later in life.

Diligence also builds confidence. Each time you complete a task responsibly, you learn that you can be trusted and that your efforts matter. You are developing a reputation for dependability, which reflects your identity in Christ. God sees every faithful step, and obedience in small matters strengthens your character more than occasional success in big things. Every time you follow through on a commitment, you honor God and prepare yourself for bigger responsibilities. Diligence and reliability are habits that last a lifetime.

*Conversation Points*

- Which commitments in your life do you consistently follow through on, and which ones need more attention?

- How can you improve diligence in small, everyday tasks at home, school, or church?

- Why is reliability an important part of godly character and trustworthiness?

- How does seeing me model diligence and reliability influence the way you approach responsibilities?

- What is one practical step you can take this week to strengthen your consistency in work or chores?

## What We're Building in These Weeks

Rest, structure, focus, and diligence are not optional habits, but vital expressions of trust in God, obedience to His Word, and worship through everyday life. Observing a Sabbath or taking intentional rest teaches reliance on God's provision and signals that true strength flows from faith, not relentless activity. Fathers carry a profound responsibility in shaping this formation. Through steady presence, quiet instruction, and modeled diligence, fathers teach that faithful effort matters more than shortcuts, that presence outweighs performance, and that obedience guides every choice.

Every hour and every task becomes an opportunity to honor God, strengthen character, and practice obedience. Sons who embrace these lessons learn that stewardship of time, attention, and work shapes men who are disciplined, trustworthy, and capable of serving God faithfully in every sphere of life.

# PART THREE:
## STEWARDSHIP OF BODY, RESOURCES, AND AUTHORITY



Faithful stewardship of the gifts God has entrusted to fathers and sons is essential to the formation of godly character. The body, possessions, and influence a man holds are not his own to use without restraint, but trusts placed in his care by the Lord. Honoring God requires the disciplined use of these gifts, reflecting obedience and confidence in His faithful provision.

Leadership and authority must likewise be understood as sacred responsibilities. Respect for God's order, careful stewardship of resources, and integrity in private and public life form the foundation of faithful leadership. Every gift, whether physical, financial, or relational, is to be used responsibly, shaping men to pursue disciplined, generous, and Christlike lives under the authority of God's Word.

♫ Scan to listen to "True North"

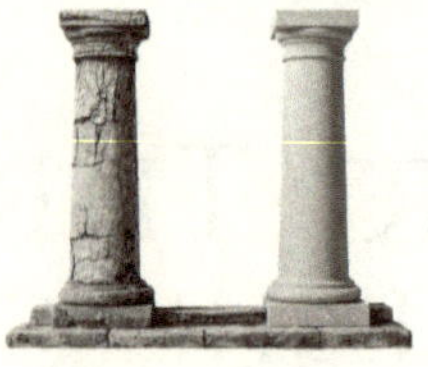



# CHAPTER 7

# PHYSICAL STEWARDSHIP: CARING FOR BODY AND PURITY

Desire itself is not evil. God created hunger, rest, enjoyment, and the longing for companionship. Yet every desire requires government. When appetite rules a man, it weakens his judgment and clouds his character. When desire is directed according to God's order, it becomes a servant rather than a master. Fathers must teach their sons that self-command over the body and mind prepares a man for responsibility, hardship, and faithful service.

Restraint and moderation belong to the formation of Christian character. A boy who learns to govern appetite, rest, and pleasure gains the strength needed to resist temptation in other areas of life. Discipline in the body trains the will. Through this instruction, fathers prepare their sons to live under the authority of God's Word, honoring Him in both private conduct and public life.

# WEEK 27: GOD'S GIFT OF HEALTH: SEEING THE BODY AS GOD'S TEMPLE

*Father's Reflection*

A father who seeks to raise a son in biblical manhood must speak plainly about the stewardship of the body. Scripture teaches us that the human body is not an accident of nature nor a possession to be used carelessly. It is entrusted to us by God and redeemed through Christ. A man, therefore, honors the Lord not only through words and worship but also through the manner in which he cares for the strength and health given to him.

Many young men grow up thinking that faith concerns only church attendance or religious language. Fathers must correct this misunderstanding. Obedience to God reaches into daily life. The way a man eats, rests, labors, and maintains his physical strength all bear witness to the seriousness with which he regards the gifts of God.

Instruction in this area begins with example. A son observes his father long before he understands his father's words. When a father maintains reasonable habits of sleep, eats with restraint, and values honest physical work, he demonstrates that discipline belongs to gratitude. These practices do not require elaborate programs. A walk taken together in the evening, labor in the yard, or steady diligence in daily responsibilities all reveal that the body was given for service rather than idleness.

A father should also explain the connection between physical stewardship and readiness for duty. Fatigue brought on by neglect weakens patience and judgment. Disorder in physical habits often leads to disorder in other areas of life. A man who refuses rest when it is needed becomes irritable and ineffective. A man who neglects his health finds it difficult to serve others with energy and clarity.

At the same time, fathers must teach balance. Physical health is not a measure of spiritual worth. Illness, weakness, and aging remain realities in a fallen world. The purpose of stewardship is not pride in strength but gratitude for what God has provided. A man cares for his body because it belongs to the Lord and because he desires to remain ready for the work God places before him.

*Scripture*

## 1 Corinthians 6:12–15 (ESV)

"All things are lawful for me," but not all things are helpful. "All things are lawful for me," but I will not be dominated by anything. "Food is meant for the stomach and the stomach for food"—and God will destroy both one and the other. The body is not meant for sexual immorality, but for the Lord, and the Lord for the body. And God raised the Lord and will also raise us up by his power. Do you not know that your bodies are members of Christ? Shall I then take the members of Christ and make them members of a prostitute? Never!

*Son's Reflection*

God gave you your body. The Bible teaches that your body belongs to God and that His Spirit lives in those who follow Christ. That means your body matters to Him.

Taking care of your health is one way to thank God for what He has given you. When you sleep well, eat wisely, stay active, and keep yourself clean, you are showing responsibility. These habits help you stay strong enough to do the work God gives you at home, at school, and in your community.

When your body is tired or neglected, it becomes harder to think clearly and harder to serve others well. A lack of rest can make you impatient. Poor habits can drain your energy. Learning to care for your body helps you stay ready for the responsibilities that come with growing up.

Think about how you treat your body during a normal week. Do your habits help you stay strong and prepared, or do they make life harder? The way you treat your health shows how seriously you take the gifts God has given you.

*Conversation Points*

- Why do you think the Bible says our bodies belong to God rather than to ourselves?

- Which daily habits help your body stay strong and healthy? Which habits make that harder?

- What are some simple ways we can care for our health as a family?

- How can physical discipline help you prepare for responsibilities in school, work, and service?

## WEEK 28: DISCIPLINE IN HABITS: ESTABLISHING CONSISTENT ROUTINES

*Father's Reflection*

The character of a man is revealed in the ordering of his ordinary days. Great decisions rarely stand alone. They arise from the habits already formed within the heart. Scripture teaches that faithfulness in small matters prepares a man for greater trust. For this reason, a father must help his son understand that discipline in daily routines carries moral weight.

A well-ordered life begins with the governance of simple practices. Rest taken at proper times, food received with moderation, and regular physical labor all contribute to the steadiness of mind and strength of body. These matters may appear humble, yet they shape a young man's readiness for responsibility. Disorder in daily living often produces disorder in judgment. The modern world often treats habit as unimportant, encouraging comfort, distraction, and indulgence. A father must resist this spirit. A boy should learn that discipline is not an enemy of freedom but its guardian. A young man who cannot govern his sleep, appetite, or use of time will struggle to govern his thoughts and actions when greater tests arrive.

Fathers teach these lessons first through example. A son watches the rhythms of his father's life. When a father rises with purpose, works diligently, and keeps reasonable order in his responsibilities, he demonstrates that discipline is part of faithful living before God. Instruction then becomes more than advice. It becomes a pattern that the son can follow.

The cultivation of steady habits prepares a young man for the burdens of adulthood. Life will present demands that require endurance, patience, and clarity of mind. A boy trained in discipline will meet those demands with greater steadiness, knowing that the strength required for larger tasks is often formed in the quiet ordering of everyday life.

*Scripture*

### 📖 1 Corinthians 9:24–27

Do you not know that in a race all the runners run, but only one receives the prize? So run that you may obtain it. Every athlete exercises self-control in all things. They do it to receive a perishable wreath, but we an imperishable. So

I do not run aimlessly; I do not box as one beating the air. But I discipline my body and keep it under control, lest after preaching to others I myself should be disqualified.

*Son's Reflection*

Many important things in life are shaped by daily habits. What you do every day, even in small ways, slowly shapes the kind of person you become.

Getting enough sleep helps you think clearly and control your attitude. Eating balanced meals gives your body the strength it needs. Regular activity keeps your body healthy and teaches you endurance. These habits may seem ordinary, but they help prepare you for school, work, and the responsibilities that will come as you grow older.

Discipline means choosing what is right even when it would be easier to ignore it. Going to bed at a reasonable time, finishing responsibilities before relaxing, and staying active instead of idle are small decisions that strengthen your character.

*Conversation Points*

- Which daily habits help you stay focused and responsible during the week?
- Which habits make it harder for you to manage school, chores, or responsibilities?
- What routines could help you sleep better, eat better, and stay active?
- How has discipline in your dad's life affected the way he handles responsibilities?

# WEEK 29: RESTRAINT IN APPETITE: PRACTICING MODERATION

## Father's Reflection

Scripture teaches that a man must learn to govern himself before he is fit to guide others. One of the earliest tests of this self-command appears in the realm of appetite. Hunger, rest, and enjoyment are not wrong in themselves. They belong to the good order of creation. Yet these desires must remain servants rather than masters. A boy who is never taught restraint soon begins to believe that every desire deserves satisfaction. This belief weakens the will and clouds judgment. When appetite rules a man, he becomes restless when denied comfort and impatient when discipline is required. A father, therefore, teaches his son that the ability to say no to himself is a mark of growing maturity.

Food provides a simple example. Meals are a gift from God, received with gratitude and moderation. Eating without restraint trains the heart toward excess rather than gratitude. A father should help his son understand that satisfaction does not require indulgence. Contentment arises from receiving what is given with thankfulness rather than seeking constant pleasure.

The same principle extends beyond food. Rest, entertainment, and leisure must also remain within proper bounds. Recreation has a rightful place in life, yet it cannot govern a young man's time or attention. When enjoyment becomes the center of life, diligence fades, and responsibility weakens.

A father's guidance in this area should be calm and steady. Discipline is not harshness. It is instruction in the proper ordering of desire. When a boy learns restraint in small matters, his character gains strength for greater trials that may come in later years.

## Scripture

### 📖 Proverbs 23: 19–21 (ESV)

Hear, my son, and be wise, and direct your heart in the way. Be not among drunkards or among gluttonous eaters of meat, for the drunkard and the glutton will come to poverty, and slumber will clothe them with rags.

## Son's Reflection

God created good things for people to enjoy. Food, rest, and recreation are part of life. These gifts are meant to be received with gratitude and used wisely.

Restraint means learning when enough is enough. A person who cannot stop eating, resting, or seeking entertainment will struggle to manage other parts of life. Self-control helps you make better decisions and remain focused on your responsibilities.

Learning restraint can be difficult. Saying no to yourself does not always feel good at first. Yet each time you practice self-control, you strengthen your ability to make wise choices in the future.

Your father helps you learn this discipline because he wants you to grow into a man who can guide his life according to what is right rather than what feels easiest.

## Conversation Points

- Why do you think self-control is important for a person's character?

- What are some situations where it can be difficult to show restraint?

- How can practicing moderation in small things prepare you for larger responsibilities?

- What habits help you remember to be thankful for what you have instead of always wanting more?

# WEEK 30: RESPECTING BOUNDARIES: HONORING GOD'S DESIGN FOR SEXUAL PURITY

*Father's Reflection*

Few responsibilities weigh more heavily upon a father than the duty to speak truthfully with his son about purity. The world often treats sexuality as a matter of impulse and entertainment. Scripture presents it in a far different light. Desire was created by God and given a rightful place within His design. When understood rightly, it belongs to the covenant of marriage and reflects the goodness of God's created order.

A father must help his son understand that desire itself is not shameful. God created men and women with purpose and dignity. Yet desire must remain under the authority of God's commands. When it is separated from that authority, it becomes destructive, damaging both the individual and others. Many voices in modern culture encourage young men to treat women as objects of amusement or conquest. Such thinking corrupts the heart and diminishes the dignity of others who bear the image of God. A father teaches his son to regard women with respect and honor, recognizing their worth before the Lord.

Purity requires discipline of both body and mind. What a young man chooses to watch, listen to, and dwell upon shapes his thoughts and attitudes. Guarding the mind is therefore an important part of honoring God's design. Fathers should speak plainly about the importance of rejecting crude language, degrading entertainment, and influences that encourage impurity.

This instruction must be given with patience and seriousness. A son should know that he can approach his father with questions or struggles without fear of ridicule or anger. Honest conversation builds trust and gives a young man guidance during years when confusion and pressure are common.

Through these conversations, fathers prepare their sons to live with integrity and respect. A young man who understands God's design for purity learns to treat both himself and others with the honor that belongs to those created in God's image.

*Scripture*

📖 **Matthew 5:27–30**

---

"You have heard that it was said, 'You shall not commit adultery.' But I say to you that everyone who looks at a woman with lustful intent has already committed adultery with her in his heart. If your right eye causes you to sin, tear it out and throw it away. For it is better that you lose one of your members than that your whole body be thrown into hell. And if your right hand causes you to sin, cut it off and throw it away. For it is better that you lose one of your members than that your whole body go into hell.

*Son's Reflection*

God created men and women with purpose and dignity. The Bible teaches that our bodies and desires are part of God's design, meant to be expressed within the covenant of marriage.

Because these desires are powerful, God gives guidance to protect us and others. Respecting boundaries means choosing thoughts, words, and actions that honor God and treat other people with dignity. What you allow into your mind matters. The shows you watch, the things you read, and the conversations you join can shape how you think about others. Choosing what is good and honorable helps protect your heart and mind.

If you ever feel confused or pressured about these matters, your father is there to guide you. Honest conversation can help you understand God's design and make wise decisions.

*Conversation Points*

- Why do you think God gives boundaries for sexuality?

- How does respecting others reflect the belief that every person is created in God's image?

- What kinds of media or influences can make it harder to maintain purity?

- How can you guard your thoughts and actions so they honor God and show respect to others?

## What We're Building in These Weeks

The body is a gift entrusted by God. Caring for physical health, therefore, becomes an act of stewardship rather than vanity. Exercise, proper rest, and balanced nourishment express gratitude for what God has given. A man who learns to govern his appetites gains strength to resist temptation in many areas of life. Self-command prepares him for responsibility in leadership, work, and service. True freedom is not the pursuit of every desire, but the ordering of desire under the authority of God's Word.

**CHAPTER 8**

# FINANCIAL STEWARDSHIP: CONTENTMENT AND GENEROSITY

Money and possessions carry moral significance. Scripture warns against the love of wealth and the restless pursuit of more, yet it also commands the faithful use of resources in service to God and neighbor. A man's relationship to material goods reveals the loyalties that govern his life. Contentment is not passive resignation. It is the deliberate recognition that God provides what is necessary for the responsibilities He assigns. A contented man receives what is given with gratitude rather than measuring his life by comparison with others.

Generosity belongs to faithful stewardship as well. Time, labor, and material resources are entrusted by God for purposes that reach beyond personal comfort. A heart shaped by contentment learns to trust God. Hands trained in generosity learn to obey Him.

## WEEK 31: LEARNING CONTENTMENT: VALUING WHAT GOD PROVIDES

*Father's Reflection*

The measure of a man's life is not discovered in the number of his possessions but in the spirit with which he receives what God has placed in his care. Contentment reflects an ordered soul. It recognizes that every provision, whether modest or abundant, comes from the hand of God and carries purpose within His providence.

The modern world presses a different message upon young men. It teaches them to measure worth by wealth, reputation, or outward display. This lesson appears in advertisements, entertainment, and the constant comparison that surrounds daily life. When a boy begins to judge his value by the possessions of others, dissatisfaction enters his heart and gratitude begins to weaken. A father must stand as a quiet counterexample to this spirit. By receiving what God provides with thanksgiving and restraint, he teaches his son that dignity does not depend upon material abundance. The young man who sees gratitude practiced in daily life learns that satisfaction arises from recognizing God's provision rather than competing for status.

Contentment does not discourage diligence. Scripture commends honest labor and responsible care for what God entrusts to a man. Yet ambition must remain governed by trust rather than by envy. A man who performs his duties with gratitude can pursue improvement without resentment toward others.

A son who learns this discipline gains a safeguard for his future. Gratitude steadies the heart when life brings seasons of scarcity or prosperity. A man who rests in God's provision carries his responsibilities with calm confidence rather than restless anxiety.

*Scripture*

Let brotherly love continue. Do not neglect to show hospitality to strangers, for thereby some have entertained angels unawares. Remember those who are in prison, as though in prison with them, and those who are mistreated, since you also are in the body. Let marriage be held in honor among all, and let the marriage bed be undefiled, for God will judge the sexually immoral and adulterous. Keep your life free from love of money, and be content with what you have, for he has said, "I will never leave you nor forsake you."

Rejoice in the Lord always; again I will say, rejoice. Let your reasonableness be known to everyone. The Lord is at hand; do not be anxious about anything, but in everything by prayer and supplication with thanksgiving let your requests be made known to God. And the peace of God, which surpasses all understanding, will guard your hearts and your minds in Christ Jesus.

### Son's Reflection

It is easy to look at what other people have and feel that you need the same things. More money, better possessions, or greater recognition can seem important when you compare yourself with others.

God teaches a different lesson. Contentment grows when you recognize what He has already provided and receive it with gratitude. Your worth does not come from what you own. It comes from being faithful with what God has entrusted to you. Contentment does not mean refusing to work hard or improve your abilities. It means doing your work with gratitude rather than envy. When you remain thankful for what you have, you can focus on developing character, skill, and responsibility.

Learning contentment now prepares you for the future. It guards your heart from envy and helps you trust God instead of chasing every desire that appears before you.

### Conversation Points

- What are some things you often want but do not truly need?

- How can you practice gratitude for what God has already provided?

- Why does comparison with others often lead to dissatisfaction?

- What examples of contentment have you seen in your father or other men you respect?

## WEEK 32: THE JOY OF GIVING: PRACTICING GENEROSITY

### Father's Reflection

A man's wealth is not determined by what he gathers but by how faithfully he directs what has been entrusted to him. Scripture teaches that generosity reflects obedience to God and concern for the well-being of others. When a man gives willingly, he acknowledges that his possessions are not ultimate possessions at all. They remain under the authority of the One who provided them.

The habit of giving begins in the home. A father who sets aside a portion of his resources for the work of the church, the care of those in need, or the support of worthy causes demonstrates that generosity belongs to the duties of faithful living. His son observes that these acts are not performed reluctantly but offered with seriousness and gratitude. A boy who participates in acts of giving begins to understand that generosity involves sacrifice. Setting aside a portion of his allowance, contributing from earnings, or offering time and labor in service teaches him that giving requires deliberate choice.

The discipline of generosity directs a young man away from selfishness and toward responsibility for the good of others. When he learns to release resources rather than cling to them, his heart becomes less vulnerable to greed and more attentive to the needs that surround him.

Generosity forms a man who understands that wealth is not an end in itself but a trust placed in his care for purposes that honor God and strengthen the community in which he lives.

### Scripture

### 📖 Proverbs 11: 25–31 (ESV)

Whoever brings blessing will be enriched, and one who waters will himself be watered. The people curse him who holds back grain, but a blessing is on the head of him who sells it. Whoever diligently seeks good seeks favor, but evil comes to him who searches for it. Whoever trusts in his riches will fall, but the righteous will flourish like a green leaf. Whoever troubles his own household will inherit the wind, and the fool will be servant to the wise of heart. The fruit of the righteous is a tree of life, and whoever captures souls is wise. If the righteous is repaid on earth, how much more the wicked and the sinner!

## Son's Reflection

Giving is one way to show that you trust God and care about other people. When you give your time, your effort, or your resources, you recognize that what you have is a gift from God.

Generosity is not only about money. You can help someone who needs assistance, volunteer your time, or share your skills with others. These actions show that you want to serve God with what He has provided. Practicing generosity also shapes your character. Each time you give, you learn to think about the needs of others instead of focusing only on yourself.

When you give faithfully, you grow into a man who uses what God provides to serve Him and help others.

## Conversation Points

- What are some ways you can give of your time, resources, or skills to help others this week?

- What examples of generosity in your family or church have influenced you most?

- How does giving shape the kind of man you are becoming?

## Week 33: Needs vs Wants: Making Wise Spending Choices Wants: Making Wise Spending Choices

*Father's Reflection*

One of the earliest financial lessons a father must teach his son is the distinction between necessity and desire. Civilizations endure when men learn to govern their appetites and weaken when desire becomes the ruler of judgment. Scripture therefore calls men to exercise discernment in the use of material resources. Needs concern the provisions required for life and responsibility. Food, shelter, clothing, and the tools necessary for honest work fall into this category. Wants arise from preference, fashion, or the influence of surrounding culture. These desires may not always be wrong, yet they must remain subject to wise judgment rather than impulse.

A boy who grows accustomed to satisfying every desire soon loses the ability to evaluate what truly matters. He becomes vulnerable to the constant pressure of novelty and comparison. Fathers must patiently guide their sons through everyday decisions, explaining why certain purchases are necessary while others must wait or be refused.

Practical instruction often occurs in ordinary circumstances. A trip to the store, the use of an allowance, or the management of small earnings provides opportunities to weigh decisions carefully. A father who explains his reasoning shows his son that wise stewardship requires thought and restraint. Patience forms an important part of this discipline. When a young man learns to wait before purchasing something he desires, he strengthens the habits of judgment and self-control. Delayed satisfaction trains the will and guards against impulsive living.

A son who learns to distinguish between needs and wants begins to understand that God faithfully provides what is necessary. This recognition deepens gratitude and prepares the heart for generosity toward others.

*Scripture*

### 📖 Luke 12:13–21 (ESV)

Someone in the crowd said to him, "Teacher, tell my brother to divide the inheritance with me." But he said to him, "Man, who made me a judge or arbitrator over you?" And he said to them, "Take care, and be on your guard against all covetousness, for one's life does not consist in the abundance of his possessions." And he told them a parable, saying, "The land of a rich man produced plentifully, and he thought to himself, 'What shall I do, for I have nowhere to store my crops?' And he said, 'I will do this: I will tear down my barns and build larger ones, and there I will store all my grain and my goods. And I will say to my soul, "Soul, you have ample goods laid up for many years; relax, eat, drink, be merry."' But God said to him, 'Fool! This night your soul is required of you, and the things you have prepared, whose will they be?' So is the one who lays up treasure for himself and is not rich toward God."

## Son's Reflection

Every day you make choices about how to spend your money, time, and attention. Some things are necessary for living and fulfilling responsibilities. Other things simply appeal to your desire for something new or exciting. Learning the difference between needs and wants helps you make wise decisions. When you pause before spending money and ask whether something is truly necessary, you avoid wasting resources on things that will not help you grow or serve others.

Waiting can also be helpful. Saving money before buying something teaches patience and responsibility. It helps you think carefully about whether something is truly worth having.

When you focus on meeting real needs first, you become better prepared to manage your resources wisely and to help others who may have less than you.

## Conversation Points

- How do you decide whether something is a need or a want?

- How can waiting or saving before buying something help you make wiser decisions?

- In what ways can careful spending create opportunities to give to others?

- How can distinguishing needs from wants shape your habits as you grow older?

## WEEK 34: AVOIDING GREED: GUARDING AGAINST MATERIALISM

*Father's Reflection*

Greed is a subtle tyrant of the heart, though it declares itself loudly in action. The desire to accumulate wealth or possessions as an end in itself erodes character, distorts judgment, and weakens confidence in God's providence. Scripture repeatedly contrasts the restless heart that chases abundance with the faithful heart that rests in God. A man who equates security or identity with material gain sets himself upon a path of anxiety, distraction, and moral compromise.

Vigilance over the desires of the heart is essential. A father must help his son discern the quiet impulses of envy, the frustration that arises when others possess more, and the endless urge to acquire what is unnecessary. Each instance provides an opportunity to reflect on God's provision, to speak gratitude aloud, and to understand that true sufficiency flows from dependence upon the Creator rather than the created. Security resides in God alone, who sustains and provides for all His children.

Avoiding greed is not an isolated discipline; it belongs to a broader life ordered under God. The man who resists the constant pull of materialism strengthens his capacity for generosity, patience, and faithful stewardship. He learns that possessions are entrusted tools, not objects of devotion, and that a heart rightly oriented toward God becomes capable of wisdom, mercy, and moral clarity in every area of life.

*Scripture*

📖 **1 Timothy 6:6–10 (ESV)**

But godliness with contentment is great gain, for we brought nothing into the world, and we cannot take anything out of the world. But if we have food and clothing, with these we will be content. But those who desire to be rich fall into temptation, into a snare, into many senseless and harmful desires that plunge people into ruin and destruction. For the love of money is a root of all kinds of evils. It is through this craving that some have wandered away from the faith and pierced themselves with many pangs.

## Son's Reflection

Greed happens when you want more than you really need, or when you start thinking that having more things makes you better, safer, or more important. God warns against this because it can quietly take over your heart and lead you to selfish choices.

Learning to avoid greed means noticing when you want something only because others have it, or because it seems easier or more fun. It also means trusting God to provide what you truly need. Being content with what you have and using it wisely is part of growing into a responsible and faithful man.

Avoiding greed is not the same as having nothing. It is about using what you have to honor God, care for others, and build your character. Practicing gratitude and generosity protects your heart from being ruled by possessions and prepares you to live with wisdom, integrity, and faithfulness.

## Conversation Points

- How do you notice greed or envy showing up in your own heart?

- Why is trust in God more secure than trust in money or possessions?

- How can generosity and contentment help protect against greed?

- What habits can help you keep your priorities focused on God rather than on acquiring more?

## What We're Building in These Weeks

Financial stewardship is inseparable from spiritual formation. A young man must first recognize God as the source of every provision, and from that recognition flows disciplined and faithful use of resources. Gratitude becomes the foundation of character, shaping responses to daily needs, cultural pressures, and the impulses of desire.

These disciplines prepare a man to live in alignment with God's Word. His relationship with money becomes a tool for worship, service, and moral formation rather than a source of pride or worry. The faithful use of resources is not optional; it is a measure of the heart and a demonstration of obedience to God.

# CHAPTER 9

# Servant Leadership: Humility, Authority, and Godly Order

True leadership is not the pursuit of power; it is an exercise of responsibility under God, rooted in humility, integrity, and service. Men who understand this truth learn that obedience to God, respect for moral and legal order, and courage in the face of challenges are inseparable from the character of a godly leader.

Christ provides the ultimate model of authority exercised in service. He taught that greatness is measured by the willingness to serve, to protect, and to sacrifice, rather than by domination or assertion. Thus, leadership demands restraint and moral courage. Excessive harshness crushes those under care, while weakness invites disorder and chaos. Leadership requires the steady alignment of action with God's Word, the humility to submit to His wisdom, and the courage to uphold what is right, even under pressure.

# Week 35: Authority as Service: Exploring Servant Leadership

## Father's Reflection

Scripture presents leadership not as a license to command, but as a sacred trust to serve. Authority entrusted to a man is an obligation to care for others, to guide with integrity, and to protect those under his oversight. Christ embodies this truth perfectly: in washing the feet of His disciples, He demonstrated that greatness is measured by humility, sacrifice, and attention to the needs of others rather than domination or assertion. Leadership exercised without this understanding risks sliding into harshness, coercion, or self-interest, or, conversely, into weakness and passivity.

Fathers bear the responsibility to model this balance. The son who witnesses his father exercising authority with measured firmness, thoughtfulness, and attentiveness to the welfare of those around him gains a concrete understanding that leadership is a moral and spiritual discipline. Every decision made in authority carries weight, shaping respect, trust, and the moral formation of others. A father's calm restraint, consistent obedience to God's Word, and discernment in moments of conflict teach that leadership is grounded in service and guided by conscience rather than impulse. The lessons of servant leadership are absorbed not only through instruction but through the lived example of a father whose authority reflects Christ's humility, courage, and care.the responsibility to model this balance. The son who witnesses his father exercising authority with measured firmness, thoughtfulness, and attentiveness to the welfare of those around him gains a concrete understanding that leadership is a moral and spiritual discipline. Every decision made in authority carries weight, shaping respect, trust, and the moral formation of others. A father's calm restraint, consistent obedience to God's Word, and discernment in moments of conflict teach that leadership is grounded in service and guided by conscience rather than impulse. The lessons of servant leadership are absorbed not only through instruction but through the lived example of a father whose authority reflects Christ's humility, courage, and care.

*Scripture*

### 📖 Philippians 2:14–18 (ESV)

Do all things without grumbling or disputing, that you may be blameless and innocent, children of God without blemish in the midst of a crooked and twisted generation, among whom you shine as lights in the world, holding fast to the word of life, so that in the day of Christ I may be proud that I did not run in vain or labor in vain. Even if I am to be poured out as a drink offering upon the sacrificial offering of your faith, I am glad and rejoice with you all. Likewise you also should be glad and rejoice with me.

*Son's Reflection*

Being a leader doesn't mean you get to boss people around. True leadership is about serving others, helping them grow, and protecting what is right. Jesus showed this by washing His disciples' feet. He led them, yet humbled Himself to care for them. That is what real authority looks like.

Leaders also control themselves. It is easy to get angry or insist on having your way, but learning to pause, think, and act wisely helps others trust you. Leadership built on service, care, and respect earns genuine authority. Watch how your dad leads. Notice when he balances firmness with kindness, guides without lording over others, and takes responsibility for his decisions. These examples show how to lead in a way that honors God and benefits those around you.

*Conversation Points*

- What does it mean to lead by serving others rather than commanding them?

- How did Jesus demonstrate leadership, and how can you follow that example?

- How does self-control relate to gaining respect as a leader?

- In what small ways can you practice serving others while taking responsibility?

# WEEK 36: MORAL COURAGE: COURAGE TO UPHOLD TRUTH

*Father's Reflection*

Moral courage is the steadfast resolve to act rightly even when opposition, ridicule, or fear threatens. It is not recklessness or the pursuit of personal acclaim, but obedience to God in the face of challenge. A man who possesses moral courage understands that fidelity to truth, justice, and righteousness carries weight beyond the immediate moment. Doing what is right often comes at personal cost, yet such resolve honors God and shapes character in a manner no comfort or applause can replicate.

Scripture presents abundant examples of moral courage. Daniel refused to compromise his convictions even under threat of death. Shadrach, Meshach, and Abednego faced the fiery furnace rather than betray God. Each account reveals that obedience frequently demands sacrifice, yet cultivates steadfastness, wisdom, and honor. Fathers must teach sons that courage is measured not in bold words, but in disciplined action grounded in conscience and Scripture.

A father's own life provides the most compelling instruction. Standing for truth in conversations, refusing compromise in household or business matters, and submitting decisions to God's authority offers a living model. Courage is quiet and deliberate. It seeks alignment with God's standards rather than the approval of men. Sons observing such integrity learn that true leadership, faithfulness, and moral influence require the courage to do what is right, even when unseen or opposed.

*Scripture*

### 📖 Psalm 37: 1–7 (ESV)

Fret not yourself because of evildoers; be not envious of wrongdoers! For they will soon fade like the grass and wither like the green herb. Trust in the Lord, and do good; dwell in the land and befriend faithfulness. Delight yourself in the Lord, and he will give you the desires of your heart. Commit your way to the Lord; trust in him, and he will act. He will bring forth your righteousness as the light, and your justice as the noonday. Be still before the Lord and wait patiently for him; fret not yourself over the one who prospers in his way, over the man who carries out evil devices!

*Son's Reflection*

Moral courage means doing what is right even when it is hard or when others do not agree. Sometimes you may feel pressure to do something wrong. Courage is choosing to obey God instead of giving in.

The Bible shows us examples. Daniel refused food that went against God's law, and Shadrach, Meshach, and Abednego would not bow to idols. They were brave because they trusted God, even when it was dangerous. You can do the same in your daily life by making honest choices, speaking truth, and standing for what is right. Each time you choose courage, you grow stronger in your ability to act rightly under pressure.

*Conversation Points*

- What situations at school, home, or with friends test your courage to do what is right?

- How does trusting God help you act courageously when it is difficult?

- What small acts of courage could you practice this week to build integrity?

- How can standing for truth even when unpopular strengthen your character?

# Week 37: Humility Before God: Leading Without Pride

## Father's Reflection

Humility is the foundation of godly leadership. Scripture repeatedly shows that leaders who succeed are those who acknowledge their limitations, seek divine guidance, and subordinate personal ambition to the welfare of others. Authority entrusted to a man is a charge, not a platform for ego. A young man who understands this truth begins to lead from a posture of service rather than self-exaltation.

Recognizing one's own insufficiency before God is the starting point of humility. A father who admits errors, seeks correction, and consults God before making decisions exemplifies leadership strengthened by restraint and wisdom. Pride fractures relationships and corrodes trust; humility enables cooperation and fosters respect for lawful order. Fathers who temper authority with gentleness demonstrate to sons that Christlike leadership is exercised with integrity, attentive to the needs of others, and guided by conscience.

Humility anchors leadership in obedience and moral clarity. It ensures that influence is exercised in alignment with God's Word rather than personal desire. Sons observing a father who balances confidence with self-restraint learn that true leadership is not about asserting power but about sustaining order, encouraging growth, and honoring God's authority in every decision.

## Scripture

### 📖 Philippians 2:1–4 (ESV)

So if there is any encouragement in Christ, any comfort from love, any participation in the Spirit, any affection and sympathy, complete my joy by being of the same mind, having the same love, being in full accord and of one mind. Do nothing from selfish ambition or conceit, but in humility count others more significant than yourselves. Let each of you look not only to his own interests, but also to the interests of others.

*Son's Reflection*

Humility means understanding that being a leader isn't about being the boss or always being right. Real strength comes from depending on God, listening to others, and admitting when you are wrong. Leaders who are humble gain respect and guide people well. Leaders who are proud often push others away or make poor choices.

You can practice humility by thinking about others before yourself, asking for advice, and admitting mistakes. Listening carefully, giving credit to others, and making decisions that help the group instead of just yourself are ways to lead humbly. Humility also helps you stay focused on God rather than praise or attention, which shapes your character and your leadership.

*Conversation Points*

- How does humility make a leader more effective?
- In what ways can you practice humility when making decisions or leading others?
- Why is admitting mistakes important for building trust and respect?
- How does depending on God guide your actions as a leader?

## WEEK 38: RESPECT AND SUBMISSION: HONORING PARENTS AND LAWFUL AUTHORITY

### *Father's Reflection*

Order and respect are inseparable from a life of obedience to God. Submission to parents, elders, and lawful authority is not weakness, but acknowledgment that God has established structures to guide, protect, and cultivate character. A son who understands this principle recognizes that obedience is rooted in reverence for God rather than mere conformity to human command.

Respect demands attentiveness, integrity, and humility of heart. A father can teach this through example: observing rules, speaking courteously, fulfilling responsibilities without complaint, and demonstrating thoughtfulness toward authority. Explaining the reasons behind expectations and rules helps sons grasp that lawful authority reflects God's moral order and serves the good of the community.

Submission must be discerning. Sons learn to evaluate instructions against Scripture, distinguishing lawful and righteous commands from those that conflict with God's standards. Fathers who model this balance, respecting authority while upholding God's law, show that obedience is an act of wisdom and a mark of maturity. Through such instruction, sons develop the discipline and discernment necessary to honor God in every sphere of life while maintaining integrity in action.

### *Scripture*

### 📖 **Ephesians 6: 1–4 (ESV)**

Children, obey your parents in the Lord, for this is right. "Honor your father and mother" (this is the first commandment with a promise), "that it may go well with you and that you may live long in the land." Fathers, do not provoke your children to anger, but bring them up in the discipline and instruction of the Lord.

### *Son's Reflection*

Respect means listening to and following the rules your parents, teachers, or leaders set, even when it is not easy. Obedience shows that you take God's order seriously and trust those He puts in authority over you. This is a sign of strength, not weakness.

You can practice respect at home by completing chores, speaking politely, and following guidance carefully. At school or in the community, following rules and treating authority with courtesy helps you grow disciplined and responsible. Doing these things even when no one is watching shows integrity. Respect and obedience teach your conscience to recognize God's authority and prepare you to lead wisely when it is your turn to guide others.

*Conversation Points*

- How can obeying parents or leaders show trust in God's order?

- What is the difference between blind obedience and thoughtful respect?

- How does practicing respect at home or school prepare you to lead responsibly?

- Can you think of a time when obeying rules strengthened trust or relationships?

# Week 39: Conscience and Integrity: Developing a God-Shaped Conscience

## Father's Reflection

A conscience shaped by God is the foundation of integrity and lasting leadership. A man whose choices are governed by divine principles acts rightly even when no one observes. Integrity and moral discernment are inseparable; obedience to God cannot be contingent on recognition, convenience, or popularity. Private moments often test the heart, yet it is precisely in these moments that conscience must be exercised. Sons who witness a father acting with consistency and honesty learn that moral authority is earned, not assumed.

Discipline of conscience cultivates both character and influence. A man whose decisions align with Scripture gains the respect of others, sustains moral credibility, and forms habits that endure under pressure. Fathers demonstrate that integrity requires deliberation, reflection, and submission to God's wisdom. Each choice made in accordance with Scripture, whether seen or unseen, shapes the man's internal compass, preparing him to navigate complexity with justice and prudence. A God-shaped conscience produces men who act rightly, serve faithfully, and uphold order, reflecting the righteousness of God in every aspect of life.

## Scripture

### 📖 Proverbs 11: 1–5 (ESV)

A false balance is an abomination to the Lord, but a just weight is his delight. When pride comes, then comes disgrace, but with the humble is wisdom. The integrity of the upright guides them, but the crookedness of the treacherous destroys them. Riches do not profit in the day of wrath, but righteousness delivers from death. The righteousness of the blameless keeps his way straight, but the wicked falls by his own wickedness.

## Son's Reflection

Your conscience is the guide inside you that tells you what is right and wrong. God gave it to help you make good choices, even when no one else is watching. Acting rightly when it's difficult shows integrity, and that builds respect and trust.

The decisions you make reveal the kind of person you are. Following your conscience helps protect you from bad habits or decisions that could grow stronger if ignored. A God-shaped conscience gives you the strength to stand firm in private and public, guiding your actions toward honesty, justice, and care for others. Practicing integrity now prepares you to be a leader whose authority is respected because it is grounded in obedience to God.

*Conversation Points*

- How can you tell whether a decision is guided by God's Word or by convenience?

- Why is it important to act rightly even when no one is watching?

- How does having integrity affect your ability to lead and serve others?

- What steps can help you strengthen your conscience and make decisions that honor God?

## What We're Building in These Weeks

True leadership is inseparable from obedience, humility, service, and moral fidelity. Sons who internalize these principles are prepared to exercise authority responsibly, lead with wisdom, serve faithfully, and honor God in every decision. Authority is not a privilege; it is stewardship, shaped by discipline, anchored in God's Word, and expressed in lives of integrity and faithful service.

# PART FOUR:
## DISCERNMENT, BROTHERHOOD, AND LEGACY

## Weeks 40–52

This section prepares sons for the wider world and the long haul of faithfulness. It emphasizes wisdom in choices, the power of godly friendships, and the call to finish well. Men learn to discern truth amid conflicting messages, to choose mentors and peers with integrity, and to stand firm under peer pressure.

♫ Scan to listen to "The Long Road of the Faithful"

# CHAPTER 10

# DISCERNMENT AND COUNSEL: WISDOM IN A NOISY WORLD

Men of faith must learn to measure every voice against the authority of Scripture. Whether evaluating advice from peers, messages from media, or the assumptions embedded in culture, God's Word remains the ultimate standard for thought and action. When a man learns to seek mentors of wisdom and humility, filter digital influences carefully, and rely upon prayer for insight, his life begins to bear the unmistakable marks of discernment.

Fathers play an essential role in cultivating this discipline. Through conversation, example, and shared reflection on Scripture, they teach sons that wisdom is not merely accumulated information but the ability to distinguish truth from error. Discernment allows a young man to move through a noisy and confusing world with steadiness, anchored not in passing opinions but in the enduring truth of God's Word.

# WEEK 40: TESTING ADVICE: PRACTICING DISCERNMENT BY COMPARING COUNSEL TO SCRIPTURE

*Father's Reflection*

The standards of the Creator do not change. A man who aspires to godly judgment must therefore learn to weigh every form of counsel against the enduring authority of God's Word. Advice is rarely neutral; it carries with it the assumptions, desires, and blind spots of the one who offers it. Scripture reminds us that wisdom is found not in accepting every opinion but in testing all things against divine truth.

For this reason, fathers should teach their sons to ask more than the simple question, "Is this good?" A wiser and deeper question is, "Does this align with God's will as revealed in Scripture?" Popularity, convenience, and immediate advantage often disguise themselves as wisdom. Yet true wisdom remains rooted in obedience to God's authority.

A father's example is often the most powerful instruction. When sons observe their fathers pausing before decisions, reflecting on Scripture, and seeking God's guidance, they begin to understand how discernment operates in daily life. Even ordinary choices can become opportunities to practice wise judgment.

Testing advice is not cynicism; it is stewardship. It guards the mind from error and protects the heart from compromise. Sons who learn to evaluate counsel through the lens of Scripture gain confidence in God's Word and develop habits of obedience that strengthen character, cultivate wisdom, and prepare them for faithful leadership.

*Scripture*

📖 **Isaiah 30:18–21 (ESV)**

Therefore the LORD will wait, that he may be gracious to you; and therefore he will be exalted, that he may have mercy on you, for the LORD is a God of justice. Blessed are all those who wait for him. For the people will dwell in Zion at Jerusalem. You will weep no more. He will surely be gracious to you at the voice of your cry. When he hears you, he will answer you. Though the Lord may give you the bread of adversity and the water of affliction, yet your teachers won't be hidden any more, but your eyes will see your teachers; and when you turn to the right hand, and when you turn to the left, your ears will hear a voice behind you, saying, "This is the way. Walk in it."

*Son's Reflection*

Not everything people say is right, even if they seem smart or popular. God wants you to check advice against His Word. Asking, "Does this match what God says?" helps you make wise choices and avoid mistakes. When someone gives advice, pause and think about it. What would Scripture say about this situation? Sometimes quick decisions lead to trouble because they ignore God's truth. Learning to test advice helps you recognize what is truly helpful and good.

You can also observe your father and other faithful men in your life. Notice how they make decisions carefully, compare them with Scripture, and consider what is right before acting. Practicing the same habit will help you grow in judgment, responsibility, and faithfulness.

*Conversation Points*

- Why is it important to compare advice to God's Word before acting?

- Can you think of a time when following someone's advice without checking Scripture caused problems?

- How can you practice testing advice in daily life, like at school or with friends?

# WEEK 41: GUARDING THE MIND: SETTING BOUNDARIES ON MEDIA AND SOCIAL INFLUENCES

## Father's Reflection

The mind is the gateway through which ideas shape belief, character, and conduct. For this reason, Scripture repeatedly urges believers to guard what enters the heart and mind. In our age, voices reach into the home through screens and devices, often carrying messages that quietly influence how we think about truth, success, identity, and virtue.

Fathers must help sons recognize that digital culture is not morally neutral. Every story, image, and message carries a vision of life. Some encourage humility, honesty, and reverence for God; others cultivate pride, envy, and confusion. Discernment requires learning to recognize these influences and to evaluate them wisely.

Guarding the mind does not mean withdrawing from the world. God has not called men to isolation, but to engagement guided by wisdom. A father who teaches his son to ask thoughtful questions equips him to navigate culture without surrendering his convictions. Questions such as, "What values does this message promote?" or "Does it encourage respect for God and others?" often reveal whether a message strengthens character or weakens it.

Practical boundaries are therefore essential. Limiting screen time, choosing wholesome content, and encouraging time spent in reading, conversation, prayer, and physical activity cultivate discipline of mind. When fathers demonstrate restraint in their own habits—showing that technology serves life rather than dominates it—sons learn that freedom lies not in endless consumption but in wise stewardship of attention.

A guarded mind preserves clarity of thought, strengthens spiritual awareness, and prepares a young man to live faithfully in a world filled with competing voices.

## Scripture

### 📖 Proverbs 4:20–27 (ESV)

> My son, attend to my words. Turn your ear to my sayings. Let them not depart from your eyes. Keep them in the center of your heart. For they are life to those who find them, and health to their whole body. Keep your heart with all diligence, for out

of it is the wellspring of life. Put away from yourself a perverse mouth. Put corrupt lips far from you. Let your eyes look straight ahead. Fix your gaze directly before you. Make the path of your feet level. Let all of your ways be established. Don't turn to the right hand nor to the left. Remove your foot from evil.

*Son's Reflection*

What you watch, read, and listen to affects how you think. If your mind is filled with messages that encourage selfishness, anger, or dishonesty, those ideas can slowly shape how you see the world. God calls us to guard our minds so that our thoughts stay focused on what is true, good, and honorable.

Guarding your mind means paying attention to the kind of media you allow into your life. Some videos, games, or social posts may seem harmless at first, but they can influence how you think about people, relationships, or success. Choosing content that encourages wisdom, kindness, and respect helps keep your mind aligned with God's truth. It also helps to pause before watching or sharing something. Ask yourself whether it helps you grow or simply distracts you. When you practice this kind of awareness, you train your mind to focus on what strengthens your character and honors God.

*Conversation Points*

- How can media influence the way people think or behave?
- What signs might show that certain content is shaping your thinking in unhealthy ways?
- How can setting limits on media use help you guard your mind?
- What kinds of activities or content help strengthen your character and focus on God's truth?

# WEEK 42: CHOOSING COUNSEL: IDENTIFYING TRUSTWORTHY MENTORS

*Father's Reflection*

No man grows in wisdom alone. The young man who surrounds himself with thoughtful and faithful voices gains stability; the one who listens carelessly to every influence risks confusion and error. Fathers, therefore, bear the responsibility of teaching their sons how to recognize trustworthy counsel and seek it with humility.

The mark of a wise mentor is not charisma or popularity but character. Such men submit their lives to the authority of God's Word. Their conduct reveals patience, integrity, restraint, and self-command. Their advice tends toward truth rather than flattery and toward correction when necessary rather than empty approval. Their goal is moral formation, not temporary comfort.

Fathers can help sons recognize such men by pointing to examples within family, church, and community—men whose lives demonstrate steady faith and reverence for God. Conversations about these examples help sons recognize the true marks of wisdom: humility, honesty, discipline, and devotion to Scripture.

Equally important is the father's willingness to seek counsel himself. When sons observe their fathers asking for advice and accepting accountability, they learn that strength is not diminished by humility. Rather, it is refined by it.

Seeking godly counsel guards against pride and isolation. A man who learns to ask for guidance develops discernment and resilience, recognizing that wisdom grows through shared experience and faithful instruction.

*Scripture*

### 📖 Proverbs 11:12–19 (ESV)

One who despises his neighbour is void of wisdom, but a man of understanding holds his peace. One who brings gossip betrays a confidence, but one who is of a trustworthy spirit is one who keeps a secret. Where there is no wise guidance, the nation falls, but in the multitude of counsellors there is victory. He who is collateral for a stranger will suffer for it, but he who refuses pledges of collateral is secure. A gracious woman obtains honour, but violent men obtain riches. Iron sharpens iron; so a man sharpens his friend's countenance. The merciful man does good to his own soul, but he who is cruel troubles his own flesh. Whoever tends the fig tree shall eat its fruit. He who looks after his master shall be honoured. Wicked people earn deceitful wages, but one who sows righteousness reaps a sure reward. Like water reflects a face, so a man's heart reflects the man.

## Son's Reflection

Everyone receives advice, but not all advice is wise or helpful. Learning to choose good counsel helps you make better decisions and avoid mistakes.

A trustworthy mentor is someone who respects God, lives honestly, and cares about helping you grow. These people tell the truth even when it is difficult, and their actions match their words. When you face a challenge or an important decision, these are the people you can turn to for guidance.

It is also important to be humble enough to ask questions and listen carefully. Seeking advice shows that you want to learn and grow. When you compare good counsel with Scripture, you gain wisdom that helps guide your choices.

## Conversation Points

- What qualities make someone a trustworthy mentor or advisor?
- Why is it important to seek guidance from people who respect God and live with integrity?
- How can listening to wise counsel protect you from poor decisions?
- Who are some people in your life that you can turn to for guidance when facing a difficult choice?

## Week 43: Wisdom from Above: Seeking God's Guidance in Every Decision

*Father's Reflection*

Human judgment, though valuable, remains incomplete. We see only a portion of reality, while God sees all things with perfect clarity. Scripture, therefore, teaches that true wisdom is not measured merely by experience or intellect, but by humble dependence upon the Lord.

A father who teaches his son that prayer and Scripture belong at the center of every serious decision is cultivating a habit that will guide him for a lifetime. Such discipline reminds a man of the limits of his own understanding and the sufficiency of God's wisdom.

Prayer directs the heart toward God. It quiets the impulse to act hastily and creates space for thoughtful reflection. Fathers can model this practice by inviting their families to pray together before important decisions. When Scripture is read and considered alongside prayer, it becomes the lens through which circumstances are interpreted and choices are evaluated. This habit produces a steadiness of character that is increasingly rare in a hurried world. A man who seeks wisdom from above is less easily swayed by the shifting opinions of the moment. His decisions grow from reflection, obedience, and trust in God's providence.

*Scripture*

### 📖 James 1:2–8 (ESV)

Count it all joy, my brothers, when you fall into various temptations, knowing that the testing of your faith produces endurance. Let endurance have its perfect work, that you may be perfect and complete, lacking in nothing. But if any of you lacks wisdom, let him ask of God, who gives to all liberally and without reproach, and it will be given to him. But let him ask in faith, without any doubting, for he who doubts is like a wave of the sea, driven by the wind and tossed. For that man shouldn't think that he will receive anything from the Lord. He is a double-minded man, unstable in all his ways.

*Son's Reflection*

Sometimes decisions can feel confusing. Friends may offer different advice, and you might not know what the right choice is. God invites you to ask Him for wisdom. Prayer is a way of speaking honestly with God and asking for help to understand what is right. Reading Scripture also helps guide your decisions. The Bible teaches principles that help you see clearly when something is wise or harmful.

When you pray and read God's Word before making important choices, you give yourself time to think carefully instead of acting quickly or following pressure from others. Asking questions like "Does this decision honor God?" helps train your heart and mind to recognize God's guidance and make choices that reflect wisdom and responsibility.

*Conversation Points*

- Why is prayer important when making decisions?

- How does Scripture help guide choices when the right answer is not immediately obvious?

- What habits can help you remember to seek God's wisdom before acting?

- How can trusting God's guidance bring peace when facing difficult decisions?

## What We're Building in These Weeks

Discernment is a lifelong discipline. Men who learn to test advice against Scripture, guard their minds from harmful influences, seek wise mentors, and pray for God's guidance develop a steady foundation for decision-making.

Rather than drifting with the changing voices of culture, they anchor their judgments in the enduring truth of God's Word. Over time, this habit forms men who think carefully, act responsibly, and lead faithfully.

# CHAPTER 11

# BROTHERHOOD AND CONVICTIONS: GODLY FRIENDSHIPS AND STANDING FIRM

The people a young man surrounds himself with influence his habits, beliefs, and direction in life. Scripture recognizes this influence and urges believers to walk with those who seek wisdom and righteousness. A young man will inevitably face moments when loyalty to God conflicts with the expectations of peers. Fathers help sons prepare for these moments by teaching them to hold firm convictions with humility and respect.

## Week 44: Choosing Friends Wisely: Valuing Integrity in Friendship

*Father's Reflection*

Friendship is rarely a neutral influence. The people a young man walks beside will shape his habits, convictions, and understanding of the world. Scripture teaches this truth plainly: Those who walk with the wise grow wiser, while careless companionship gradually pulls a man away from what is good.

True friendship is not merely built upon shared interests or convenience. It is a relationship of mutual influence, where character quietly passes from one life to another. Over time, the habits, attitudes, and beliefs of those closest to us begin to shape our own.

Wise friendships are rooted in character. Men who pursue integrity, humility, and reverence for God tend to encourage the same qualities in those around them. Such companions offer encouragement in moments of weakness and honest counsel when a man begins to drift. Their influence is steady and strengthening, like iron sharpening iron.

Not every friendship will be easy or entertaining. Some of the most valuable companions are those who challenge us to grow and who quietly remind us of what is right. These relationships shape a young man's moral imagination, helping him see the beauty of a life ordered by truth and virtue.

Fathers can guide sons by pointing to examples of trustworthy companions and by reminding them that friendship requires responsibility. A young man should not only seek good friends but also strive to become one himself. When friendship is built upon integrity and shared devotion to what is good, it becomes a powerful source of encouragement and stability throughout life.

*Scripture*

### 📖 1 Corinthians 15:29–34 (ESV)

Or else what will they do who are baptised for the dead? If the dead aren't raised at all, why then are they baptised for the dead? Why do we also stand in jeopardy every hour? I affirm, by the boasting in you which I have in Christ Jesus our Lord, I die daily. If I fought with animals at Ephesus for human purposes, what does it profit me? If the dead are not raised, then "let's eat and drink, for tomorrow we die." Don't be deceived! "Evil companionships corrupt good morals." Wake up righteously, and don't sin, for some have no knowledge of God. I say this to your shame.

*Son's Reflection*

Friends have a big influence on the way you think and act. Spending time with people who make wise choices can help you grow in good habits and strong character. Being around people who ignore what is right can slowly lead you toward poor decisions.

Choosing friends wisely means paying attention to their character. Do they treat others with respect? Do they try to do what is right, even when it is difficult? Friends who value honesty, kindness, and responsibility will encourage those same qualities in you. Friendship also goes both ways. Being a good friend means supporting others, telling the truth, and encouraging them to make wise choices. When you choose friends who share these values, your friendships become stronger and help you grow into the person God wants you to be.

*Conversation Points*

- What qualities make someone a trustworthy and wise friend?

- How can friends influence the choices we make each day?

- Why is character more important than shared interests when choosing close friends?

- How can you become the kind of friend who encourages others to do what is right?

## Week 45: Loyalty and Accountability: Faithfulness in Friendship

*Father's Reflection*

Friendship reveals its true character not during moments of ease, but during seasons of difficulty. Loyalty is often misunderstood as simply standing beside a friend no matter what he does. Scripture presents a deeper picture. True loyalty seeks the good of another person, even when that requires honesty or correction.

Faithful friends strengthen one another through encouragement, truth, and accountability. They celebrate one another's successes but also speak when a companion begins to wander from wisdom. Such honesty requires courage and humility. A friend who quietly allows destructive habits to grow is not acting in loyalty but in neglect. At times, a loyal friend must offer words that are uncomfortable but necessary. Spoken with humility and genuine care, such words can guide a companion back toward wisdom.

Shared difficulties often deepen friendship more than shared entertainment ever could. When friends remain present during hardship, disappointment, or failure, they demonstrate a faithfulness that reflects the steadfastness praised throughout Scripture.

Fathers should help sons understand that faithful friendships are among life's great blessings. They are not only sources of companionship but also partners in the lifelong pursuit of wisdom and virtue.

*Scripture*

### 📖 Ecclesiastes 4:9–12 (ESV)

Two are better than one, because they have a good reward for their labor. For if they fall, the one will lift up his fellow; but woe to him who is alone when he falls, and doesn't have another to lift him up. Again, if two lie together, then they have warmth; but how can one keep warm alone? If a man prevails against one who is alone, two shall withstand him; and a threefold cord is not quickly broken.

## Son's Reflection

A true friend stays loyal when things are difficult. This means helping each other, encouraging each other, and standing together when challenges come. Friends who support one another in tough moments build strong and lasting relationships.

Loyalty also means helping a friend stay on the right path. If a friend starts making poor choices, being a good friend may mean speaking honestly and encouraging them to change. This can feel uncomfortable, but real friendship cares about what is right. When friends are both loyal and honest, they help each other grow stronger. These friendships become places where trust grows, where challenges are faced together, and where both people are encouraged to become wiser and more faithful.

## Conversation Points

- What does loyalty in friendship really mean?
- Why can honest correction sometimes be an important part of being a good friend?
- How do difficult experiences strengthen true friendships?
- How can you show loyalty to your friends in everyday situations?

# WEEK 46: SPEAKING TRUTH IN LOVE: HANDLING CONFLICT WITH HONESTY AND GRACE

*Father's Reflection*

Disagreement is inevitable wherever people share life closely. Conflict itself is not the danger; the danger arises when pride, anger, or silence replaces honest conversation. Scripture calls believers to speak truth with humility and love. The purpose of honest correction is never to win an argument but to restore peace and strengthen trust. When handled with wisdom, even difficult conversations can deepen a friendship.

A father can teach his son that confronting a problem with a friend requires patience and careful words. Harsh correction can wound unnecessarily, while avoiding the issue entirely allows resentment to grow beneath the surface. Wisdom lies in addressing concerns clearly while maintaining respect and kindness.

Humility must guide every step. Before correcting another, a man must first examine his own conduct. Such humility prevents pride from poisoning the conversation and keeps the focus on restoration rather than blame.

Handled well, conflict becomes an opportunity to practice maturity, forgiveness, and grace.

*Scripture*

### 📖 Matthew 18:15–20 (ESV)

"If your brother sins against you, go, show him his fault between you and him alone. If he listens to you, you have gained back your brother. But if he doesn't listen, take one or two more with you, that at the mouth of two or three witnesses every word may be established. If he refuses to listen to them, tell it to the assembly. If he refuses to hear the assembly also, let him be to you as a Gentile or a tax collector. Most certainly I tell you, whatever things you bind on earth will have been bound in heaven, and whatever things you release on earth will have been released in heaven. Again, assuredly I tell you, that if two of you will agree on earth concerning anything that they will ask, it will be done for them by my Father who is in heaven. For where two or three are gathered together in my name, there I am in the middle of them."

*Son's Reflection*

Sometimes friends disagree or hurt each other's feelings. When that happens, it is important to deal with the problem instead of ignoring it. Talking honestly and kindly can help repair the friendship. Speaking truth in love means telling the truth without trying to embarrass or attack the other person. It means explaining how you feel, listening carefully, and being willing to forgive when mistakes happen.

When friends handle disagreements with patience and honesty, their friendship often becomes stronger than before.

*Conversation Points*

- Why is it important to address problems in friendships instead of ignoring them?

- How can someone speak honestly without being hurtful?

- Why is listening important when resolving disagreements?

- How can forgiveness help repair a friendship after conflict?

# Week 47: Courage to Stand Alone: Resisting Negative Peer Pressure

## Father's Reflection

Every young man eventually faces moments when the expectations of friends conflict with his convictions. These moments quietly reveal character. Courage is not always dramatic; often it appears in the quiet strength to decline what is wrong. Standing apart from the crowd requires both clarity and composure. Convictions rooted in Scripture provide the confidence to refuse harmful choices without anger or arrogance. A man who understands what he believes and why he believes it is far less easily swayed by the approval of others.

It is also important to remember that a man who stands with God is never truly alone. Faithful friends, mentors, and family provide support and encouragement during difficult moments.

When a young man learns to ground his identity in truth rather than popularity, he gains a steady independence of mind. Such men are able to walk faithfully even when the path requires standing apart from the crowd.

## Scripture

### 📖 Romans 12:1–3 (ESV)

Therefore I urge you, brothers, by the mercies of God, to present your bodies a living sacrifice, holy, acceptable to God, which is your spiritual service. Don't be conformed to this world, but be transformed by the renewing of your mind, so that you may prove what is the good, well-pleasing, and perfect will of God. For I say through the grace that was given me, to every man who is amongst you, not to think of himself more highly than he ought to think; but to think reasonably, as God has apportioned to each person a measure of faith.

## Son's Reflection

Sometimes friends or classmates may pressure you to do something you know is wrong. This could be teasing someone, breaking rules, or making choices that go against what you believe.

In those moments, courage means choosing what is right even if others disagree.

You do not have to respond with anger or argument. Often, you can simply say that it isn't something you want to do or that it goes against your values. Speaking calmly and confidently often earns respect, even if others do not agree.

It also helps to stay close to friends who share your desire to do what is right. When you surround yourself with people who respect your convictions, it becomes easier to stand firm.

Choosing integrity over approval builds strength of character and helps you remain faithful to what God teaches.

## Conversation Points

- Why can peer pressure make it difficult to do what is right?

- What are some respectful ways to decline a bad suggestion from friends?

- How can having supportive friends make it easier to stand firm in your convictions?

- Why is integrity more important than gaining approval from others?

## What We're Building in These Weeks

Friendship holds remarkable power in shaping a young man's life. The companions he chooses will influence his habits, beliefs, and direction for years to come. By learning to choose friends wisely, practice loyalty and accountability, speak truth with humility, and stand firm under pressure, young men develop friendships that strengthen rather than weaken their character.

These lessons cultivate discernment, courage, and integrity. Over time, they prepare a young man to build relationships that encourage faithfulness, deepen wisdom, and help him live a life that honors God.

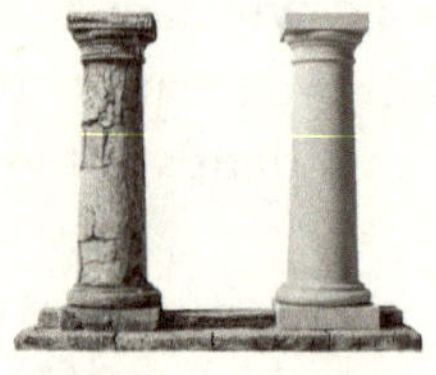

**CHAPTER 12**

# LEGACY AND FAITHFULNESS: FINISHING WELL WITH INTEGRITY

Life unfolds through many seasons: growth and struggle, triumph and disappointment. Through each of these seasons, the measure of a man's character is not popularity or recognition, but steady obedience to God. The quiet habits formed in youth become the foundation for a lifetime of faithful living. Integrity practiced in private prepares a man to serve faithfully in public. Trials refine courage and deepen trust in God's providence. And the example of one faithful life often influences generations yet to come.

The weeks in this final section encourage fathers and sons to reflect on the enduring nature of character. Faithfulness is rarely dramatic. It is built through daily choices, patient perseverance, and devotion to God in both visible and hidden moments.

# Week 48: Invisible Integrity: Honoring God When No One Is Watching

## *Father's Reflection*

Public recognition may acknowledge virtue, but private discipline is what sustains it. Scripture reminds us that God sees what is hidden and values faithfulness even in the smallest duties. A man who honors God when no one is watching develops a conscience that remains steady regardless of circumstance. His character is not dependent on applause or recognition, because the true audience of his life is the Lord.

Invisible integrity is formed through the quiet consistency of daily habits. The discipline of prayer when the house is silent, honesty in work when no supervisor is present, and careful attention to responsibilities that bring no praise all reveal the true condition of a man's heart. These quiet acts rarely draw attention, yet over time they shape a life of remarkable strength. Character is not forged in moments of visibility but in the countless ordinary decisions that occur when no one else is present.

For a father, this truth carries particular weight. Sons observe far more than they are formally taught. They notice whether their father speaks truthfully, whether he keeps his promises, and whether his private conduct matches his public words. When a son sees consistency between what his father professes and how he lives, a powerful lesson is quietly communicated. He learns that integrity is not a performance but a way of life.

Invisible integrity also protects the heart from hypocrisy. When a man's inner life aligns with his outward actions, his character becomes unified and trustworthy. There is no need to maintain separate versions of himself for different audiences. Such wholeness brings a quiet confidence that endures through changing circumstances.

In many ways, the habits formed in hidden places determine the strength of a man's public life. Sons who learn to honor God in these unseen moments are preparing themselves for responsibilities that will come later. Leadership, influence, and trust are rarely granted suddenly; they grow naturally from a life that has been shaped by faithfulness in small things.

A father who models this quiet integrity offers his son one of the greatest gifts possible: the example of a life lived consistently before God. Over time, the son learns that greatness in God's kingdom is not measured by spectacle or recognition, but by steady fidelity in every circumstance.

*Scripture*

### 📖 Matthew 6: 1–4 (ESV)

"Be careful that you don't do your charitable giving before men, to be seen by them, or else you have no reward from your Father who is in heaven. Therefore when you do merciful deeds, don't sound a trumpet before yourself, as the hypocrites do in the synagogues and in the streets, that they may get glory from men. Most certainly I tell you, they have received their reward. But when you do merciful deeds, don't let your left hand know what your right hand does, so that your merciful deeds may be in secret, then your Father who sees in secret will reward you openly.

*Son's Reflection*

Many of the choices that shape your character happen when no one else is watching. Being honest with homework, completing chores carefully, or keeping a promise even when it would be easy to ignore it are all examples of integrity.

God sees these quiet moments and values them. Developing habits such as prayer, reading Scripture, and doing your work faithfully helps you grow into a person who can be trusted.

These habits may seem small now, but they build strength in your character over time. When you choose to do what is right in private, you prepare yourself to act with courage and honesty in public situations as well. Invisible integrity becomes the foundation for a life that honors God.

*Conversation Points*

- Why are small, unseen choices important for building character?

- How can personal prayer and devotion strengthen integrity?

- What are some daily habits that help develop honesty and responsibility?

- Why does God value faithfulness even when others do not notice it?

## WEEK 49: PASSING THE TORCH: TEACHING THE NEXT GENERATION

*Father's Reflection*

Faith was never intended to remain confined within a single life. From the earliest pages of Scripture, God's truth is presented as a living inheritance passed from one generation to the next. Fathers and mothers receive the gift of faith, nurture it within their own lives, and then faithfully pass it forward so that the knowledge of God continues beyond their own years.

For fathers, this calling carries particular responsibility. A father's words, habits, and priorities communicate powerful lessons about what truly matters in life. Whether intentionally or not, every father is shaping the spiritual understanding of his children. The question is not whether influence will occur, but what kind of influence it will be.

Teaching the next generation rarely happens through formal instruction alone. It unfolds through everyday moments—conversations at the dinner table, prayers spoken before sleep, reflections during times of difficulty, and simple reminders of God's goodness throughout daily life. Faith becomes real to a son when he sees it woven naturally into the rhythm of family life.

Stories play an especially powerful role in this process. When fathers share accounts of God's faithfulness—both from Scripture and from their own lives—they help sons see that faith is not an abstract idea but a living reality. Stories of perseverance, answered prayer, repentance, and renewal allow a young man to understand that God has been at work long before his own generation arrived.

Equally important is honesty. Sons benefit from hearing not only about moments of strength but also about times when faith required humility, repentance, or renewed trust in God. Such honesty demonstrates that faithfulness does not require perfection; it requires a heart that continually turns back to God.

Passing the torch of faith also means preparing sons to become future guides for others. The lessons a father teaches today will one day influence grandchildren, communities, and lives that he may never personally meet. This generational vision helps fathers recognize the lasting significance of their daily efforts.

When a father faithfully teaches, listens, and walks alongside his son in matters of faith, he becomes part of a long chain of spiritual inheritance stretching backward through history and forward into the future. In time, the son who receives this inheritance will carry the same responsibility, passing forward the truth that was once entrusted to him.

*Scripture*

## 📖 Deuteronomy 6:5–9 (ESV)

You shall love the LORD your God with all your heart, with all your soul, and with all your might. These words, which I command you today, shall be on your heart; and you shall teach them diligently to your children, and shall talk of them when you sit in your house, and when you walk by the way, and when you lie down, and when you rise up. You shall bind them for a sign on your hand, and they shall be for frontlets between your eyes. You shall write them on the door posts of your house and on your gates.

*Son's Reflection*

Faith grows stronger when it is shared. The things you learn about God today can help guide others in the future. Listening to stories from your family or from the Bible helps you understand how faith has shaped people's lives across many generations. These stories remind us that faith is not only personal, but also something that connects us with those who came before us and those who will come after.

You can also practice sharing what you learn with others. Encouraging a younger sibling, helping a friend understand something you learned in church, or explaining why your faith matters to you are simple ways of passing truth forward.

When you value what has been taught to you and share it with others, you become part of a chain of faith stretching from the past into the future.

*Conversation Points*

- Why is it important for each generation to teach the next about faith?

- What stories from your family or Scripture inspire perseverance?

- How can sharing experiences strengthen someone else's faith?

- In what ways might you encourage others with what you are learning?

# WEEK 50: ENDURING FAITH: PERSEVERING THROUGH TRIALS

## Father's Reflection

A life of faith inevitably encounters seasons of hardship. No family, no matter how devoted to God, is exempt from difficulty. Trials may appear in the form of disappointment, loss, conflict, uncertainty, or circumstances that seem beyond one's control. Yet Scripture consistently teaches us that these seasons are not meaningless interruptions in the life of faith. Rather, they are instruments through which character is refined and spiritual maturity is strengthened.

Endurance in adversity deepens trust in God's providence. When life unfolds according to our expectations, faith can remain largely untested. It is in moments of difficulty that the foundations of belief are revealed. Trials invite believers to rely more fully on God's wisdom rather than their own understanding.

Fathers play an important role in helping sons interpret these seasons wisely. A young man may be tempted to assume that hardship signals failure or abandonment. Yet Scripture offers a different perspective. Many of the most faithful men and women in the Bible endured profound trials. Their stories remind us that difficulty is often the context in which God accomplishes some of His most meaningful work.

A father's response to hardship speaks with quiet authority. When sons observe patience in the midst of frustration, prayer in moments of uncertainty, and steady trust during difficult circumstances, they learn lessons that cannot easily be taught through words alone. They discover that resilience is not the absence of hardship but the determination to remain faithful in the midst of it.

Such endurance builds a deeper and more durable faith. Over time, trials that once seemed overwhelming become testimonies of God's sustaining grace. They remind a family that God's purposes often extend beyond immediate understanding.

When fathers guide their sons through these seasons with calm faith and steady hope, they help prepare them for the inevitable challenges of adulthood. The young man who learns to trust God during adversity will carry that strength into every future responsibility he faces.

In this way, hardship becomes not merely something to endure but a training ground where courage, patience, and lasting faith are formed.

*Scripture*

### 📖 Hebrews 12: 7–11 (ESV)

It is for discipline that you endure. God deals with you as with children, for what son is there whom his father doesn't discipline? But if you are without discipline, of which all have been made partakers, then you are illegitimate, and not children. Furthermore, we had the fathers of our flesh to chasten us, and we paid them respect. Shall we not much rather be in subjection to the Father of spirits, and live? For they indeed, for a few days, punished us as seemed good to them; but he for our profit, that we may be partakers of his holiness. All chastening seems for the present to be not joyous but grievous; yet afterward it yields the peaceful fruit of righteousness to those who have been trained by it.

*Son's Reflection*

Everyone faces difficult moments. These might include disappointment, frustration, or problems that take time to solve. The Bible teaches that these experiences can help strengthen your faith and character. Instead of giving up when something is hard, you can ask God for strength and guidance. Talking with your father, mentors, or trusted friends can also help you stay encouraged during difficult times.

When you continue doing what is right even when it is challenging, you build perseverance. Over time, these experiences help you grow stronger, wiser, and more confident in God's care.

*Conversation Points*

- Why can challenges help strengthen a person's character?
- How can prayer and faith help during difficult situations?
- What examples from Scripture show people enduring trials faithfully?
- How can perseverance today prepare you for future challenges?

## WEEK 51: THE LONG VIEW OF SUCCESS: REDEFINING ACHIEVEMENT

*Father's Reflection*

Modern culture often defines success through visibility, drawing admiration from others. These measures dominate public conversation, shaping how many people evaluate their lives and their worth. Yet Scripture presents a profoundly different understanding of success.

In God's kingdom, success is measured primarily by faithfulness. A man who lives in obedience to God, fulfills his responsibilities with diligence, and treats others with humility is living a successful life, even if his achievements never receive public recognition.

This perspective requires a longer view of life. Many accomplishments that appear impressive in the moment quickly fade with time. Titles change, recognition passes to others, and worldly accomplishments often lose their significance. In contrast, the quiet influence of faithful living continues long after public attention has shifted elsewhere.

Fathers have an important opportunity to guide sons toward this broader understanding. By discussing the difference between appearance and substance, they help young men develop wisdom about the kind of life that truly matters. A father can explain that integrity, reliability, generosity, and devotion to God create a legacy that no temporary success can equal.

The steady fulfillment of daily duties often appears ordinary, yet it forms the foundation of a life that honors God. Caring for family, serving faithfully in one's work, helping others in need, and maintaining a humble heart before God are all expressions of genuine success.

Teaching sons to value faithfulness over recognition protects them from two common dangers: discouragement and pride. When success is defined by public approval, disappointment becomes inevitable, and pride easily follows achievement. But when success is measured by obedience to God, a man gains freedom. He can pursue excellence without becoming captive to the opinions of others.

A young man who embraces this perspective learns to invest his energy in what truly endures. He becomes less concerned with comparison and more focused on living faithfully before God. Over time, this quiet commitment produces a life of deep purpose and lasting influence.

*Scripture*

### 📖 Matthew 6: 25–32 (ESV)

Therefore I tell you, don't be anxious for your life: what you will eat, or what you will drink; nor yet for your body, what you will wear. Isn't life more than food, and the body more than clothing? See the birds of the sky, that they don't sow, neither do they reap, nor gather into barns. Your heavenly Father feeds them. Aren't you of much more value than they? "Which of you, by being anxious, can add one moment to his lifespan? Why are you anxious about clothing? Consider the lilies of the field, how they grow. They don't toil, neither do they spin, yet I tell you that even Solomon in all his glory was not dressed like one of these. But if God so clothes the grass of the field, which today exists, and tomorrow is thrown into the oven, won't he much more clothe you, you of little faith? "Therefore don't be anxious, saying, 'What will we eat?', 'What will we drink?' or, 'With what will we be clothed?' For the Gentiles seek after all these things; for your heavenly Father knows that you need all these things.

*Son's Reflection*

Many people think success means being famous, wealthy, or admired by others. But God sees success differently. He values faithfulness. Doing what is right, working diligently, and honoring God with your choices are true measures of success. You may not always receive recognition for doing the right thing, but those choices still matter. Helping others, completing your work responsibly, and staying committed to your values are examples of faithful living. When you focus on honoring God rather than impressing others, you develop a deeper sense of purpose. This kind of success lasts much longer than popularity or awards.

*Conversation Points*

- How does God's definition of success differ from the world's?

- Why is faithfulness more lasting than popularity or recognition?

- How can focusing on obedience change the way you approach work or responsibilities?

- What habits help build a life centered on faithfulness?

## Week 52: Finishing Well: Celebrating a Life of Faithfulness

*Father's Reflection*

Every life moves steadily toward its conclusion. Though daily responsibilities often occupy our attention, Scripture reminds us that life is ultimately a journey with an eternal destination. For this reason, believers are encouraged not merely to begin well but to finish well—to persevere in faith, humility, and devotion until the final chapter of life.

Finishing well is not the result of a single decision made late in life. It is the natural outcome of many years of steady faithfulness. Each small act of obedience, each moment of repentance, each quiet prayer, and each decision to trust God contributes to the direction a life ultimately takes.

Fathers who reflect on this truth help their sons understand that character is formed gradually. A man does not suddenly become faithful near the end of his life; rather, he becomes faithful through the accumulation of countless choices made across many years.

Both Scripture and history offer examples of individuals who remained devoted to God through long seasons of service. Their lives were rarely defined by dramatic achievements alone. More often, they were marked by patient perseverance, quiet acts of service, and enduring trust in God's providence. These men and women demonstrate that faithfulness across a lifetime leaves a far deeper legacy than moments of temporary recognition.

Such lives influence far more than the individuals who live them. A father's example shapes his children. Those children may carry the same faith into their own families. In time, the quiet faithfulness of one generation may influence communities and descendants far beyond anything the original father imagined.

As this year of reflection draws to a close, fathers and sons have an opportunity to look back with gratitude. The conversations shared, the prayers offered, and the lessons discussed are seeds planted in fertile soil. Though their full impact may not yet be visible, they will continue to grow in the years ahead.

A life lived faithfully before God honors Him in every season. It also leaves behind a legacy that endures far beyond a single lifetime. When a father guides his son toward that kind of life, he participates in a work whose influence may extend for generations to come.

*Scripture*

📖 **Philippians 1: 27–30 (ESV)**

Only let your manner of life be worthy of the gospel of Christ, so that whether I come and see you or am absent, I may hear of you that you are standing firm in one spirit, with one mind striving side by side for the faith of the gospel, and not frightened in anything by your opponents. This is a clear sign to them of their destruction, but of your salvation, and that from God. For it has been granted to you that for the sake of Christ you should not only believe in him but also suffer for his sake, engaged in the same conflict that you saw I had and now hear that I still have.

*Son's Reflection*

Life is a long journey, and the goal is to remain faithful to God from beginning to end. The habits you build now help prepare you to live that kind of life. Finishing well means continuing to trust God even when life changes or becomes difficult. Each small act of faithfulness becomes part of a larger story that shapes who you become. As you grow older, you will have opportunities to guide others just as your father has guided you. The lessons you learn now can help you live a life that honors God and encourages others for many years to come.

*Conversation Points*

- What does it mean to "finish well" in a life of faith?
- How can the habits you develop now influence your future?
- Why is consistency over time important in building a strong character?
- How might your faithfulness today influence others in the future?

## What We're Building in These Weeks

Faithfulness is the quiet strength that sustains a life devoted to God. Through integrity practiced in private, perseverance in trials, wise understanding of success, and the commitment to pass faith to others, sons are prepared to live with purpose and conviction. The hope set before them is simple yet profound: A life lived steadily in obedience to God will bear fruit far beyond the present moment, leaving a legacy of faith that endures for generations.

# Conclusion

Through these weeks of conversation, reflection, and prayer, fathers have been encouraged to lead not with perfection but with presence. A father who embraces this calling with humility and perseverance becomes a steady guide in his son's life. Each moment invested in spiritual formation builds a legacy that extends far beyond the present. In guiding your son toward Christ-centered manhood, you participate in a work that reaches across generations. Character formed today often shapes families, communities, and lives that a father may never personally see.

Choosing to invest in the spiritual formation of your son is no small decision. It requires time, humility, and the willingness to begin again when conversations feel awkward or schedules become crowded. Yet the very act of stepping into this responsibility reflects courage and conviction.

If you have walked through these weeks with sincerity, you have already taken an important step toward shaping a legacy of faith within your family. The prayers you have spoken, the questions you have discussed, and the moments you have shared together contribute to a foundation that will continue influencing your son long after this book has been closed. This devotional has offered a structured year of reflection and conversation, but it is meant to be a beginning rather than a conclusion. The work of spiritual fatherhood continues throughout every stage of life. Sons grow, questions deepen, and new challenges arise. Each season invites fathers to continue learning, guiding, and growing alongside their children.

Before closing this book, pause for a moment of reflection. Consider what you have learned, the conversations you have shared with your son, and the habits you have begun to establish together.

Ask yourself what the next step might be. Perhaps it is beginning or renewing a regular devotional time together. Perhaps it is committing to greater patience in your conversations, or embracing more fully the role of servant leadership within your family.

Whatever that step may be, bring it before God in prayer. Ask for wisdom, strength, and perseverance as you continue guiding your son toward maturity, character, and faithful devotion.

If the ideas and reflections in this book have encouraged you, we invite you to explore other resources from Oak & Anchor Press. Our mission is to publish works that strengthen faith, cultivate character, and support families seeking to live with conviction and purpose.

You can discover additional books and resources designed for spiritual formation by visiting oakanchorpress.com. While there, we also invite you to subscribe to the Oak & Anchor Newsletter, where you will receive updates on new publications, reflections on faith and culture, and resources to support fathers, families, and communities seeking to build lives of enduring faithfulness.

# THANK YOU FOR WALKING THIS ROAD TOGETHER.

WHAT HAS BEEN BUILT HERE
IS MEANT TO ENDURE.

IF THIS TIME HAS STRENGTHENED YOU, CONSIDER:

 Exploring more from Oak & Anchor

 Sharing this with another father and son

 Leaving a review to guide others here

♪ Scan to listen to *"Built for More"*

# OAK & ANCHOR PRESS

OAKANCHORPRESS.COM